PHONICS SKILLS & STRATEGIES

in a Balanced Reading Program

by Dorothy Rubin, Ph.D.
The College of New Jersey

Fearon Teacher Aids
A Division of Frank Schaffer Publications, Inc.

Dedication

With love to my supportive and understanding
husband, Artie,
my precious daughters, Carol and Sharon,
my delightful grandchildren, Jennifer,
Andrew, Melissa, and Kelsey,
and my considerate and charming son-in-law, Seth.

Senior Editor: Kristin Eclov

Editor: Lisa Schwimmer Marier

Copyeditor: Lisa Schwimmer Marier

Cover and Interior Design: RedLane Studio

Illustration: Ray Barton

Cover Illustration: Jack Lindstrom, FAB Artists

© Fearon Teacher Aids

A Division of Frank Schaffer Publications, Inc.
23740 Hawthorne Boulevard
Torrance, CA 90505-5927

FE7970
ISBN 0-7682-0048-2

Contents

Contents

About This Resource

Phonics: Skills and Strategies in a Balanced Reading Program, Level 4 is the last in a series of four phonics skills books. This series, which is intended to be a valuable resource for parents and teachers, contains a wealth of challenging, stimulating, and necessary reading skills and strategies for young students. The wide variety of materials will help parents and teachers as they work with students of all ability levels. This excellent reading resource is published in a format that includes practice pages that are easily reproducible for distribution to children in classrooms or at home—an important time-saver for busy teachers and parents.*

Phonics: Skills and Strategies in a Balanced Reading Program is for anyone who is interested in helping children gain the skills and strategies they need to become proficient readers. Most information is still passed through the written word, and anyone who finds reading difficult is seriously handicapped in the civilized struggle for a place in the world. Children who come from homes surrounded by print material usually do better in reading, and subsequently in school achievement, than children who do not come from such environments.

Reading is a thinking act. However, without the ability to identify words on the printed page, there is no reading. Word recognition, which is the foundation of reading, consists of the pronunciation and meaning strategies that are necessary to figure out printed words. And phonics, which is part of word recognition, is especially important because it helps students gain self-reliance in reading. *Phonics: Skills and Strategies in a Balanced Reading Program* recognizes that phonics instruction in the early grades is essential and should be taught in conjunction with meaning.

This resource is the fourth level in the *Phonics: Skills and Strategies in a Balanced Reading Program* series. It is based on graduated levels of difficulty and presents a sequential development of phonics skills and strategies. All four books in this series are published in a format that includes practice pages and "Skinny Books." Each Skinny Book is a short, illustrated story related to the presented skills. These small books are reproducible and easy to assemble for distribution to children in classrooms or at home. The books are not only important time-savers for busy teachers, but also important aids for parents who want to help their children succeed in learning to read.

Whom This Resource Is For

The materials in *Phonics: Skills and Strategies in a Balanced Reading Program* are designed for students in the primary grades (K–3), but can be used with any

---

* Individual student practice-exercise workbooks that include the Skinny Books are available in separate packages. Please see your teacher resource dealer or contact the publisher directly.

students who need to gain independence in figuring out words from the printed page. The emphasis throughout is on engaging children in activities that will help them to become good strategic readers.

Studies strongly suggest that "reading skill may not be developed as quickly or as well in the primary grades as is believed," and that "we are just beginning to detect the dire consequences that a poor initial start with reading has on later development." (From Connie Juel's "Beginning Reading" in *Handbook of Reading Research*, Vol. II, Rebecca Barr, Michael L. Kamil, Peter Mosenthal, and P. David Pearson, eds., New York: Longman, 1991, p. 759.) This phonics resource will help ensure parents and primary-grade teachers that their students are gaining the phonics skills and strategies they need to become good readers and ultimately to succeed in school.

Each book in this series helps raise students' test scores in a variety of areas. It can help students improve their scores on standardized achievement and basic skills tests, as well as on teacher-generated tests.

The *Phonics: Skills and Strategies in a Balanced Reading Program* series, as well as *Comprehension Skills and Strategies in a Balanced Reading Program* and *Vocabulary Skills and Strategies in a Balanced Reading Program,* help students achieve better in all subject-matter areas. All of these books also start students on the road to preparing for the Scholastic Assessment Test (SAT).

The Organization

The *Phonics: Skills and Strategies in a Balanced Reading Program* series is organized into the following four levels and can be used in the primary grades (K–3) based on children's individual differences.

Level 1 Phonics:	Beginning Skills and Strategies
Level 2 Phonics:	Extending Skills and Strategies
Level 3 Phonics:	Perfecting Skills and Strategies
Level 4 Phonics:	Advanced Skills and Strategies

This resource, Level 4, contains three skill areas—special letters and sounds, syllabication, and word families (phonograms). Each skill and strategy section includes accompanying teaching material, learning objectives, special activities, student practice sheets, and a skinny reading book. The teaching material precedes the practices and contains the following:

Explanation
Teaching Strategies in Action
    Sample Practices
    Modeling Strategy
Learning Objectives
Directions for Student Activities and Practices
Extensions
Assessment Tool Progress Report

The extension activities in the teaching materials are intended to extend learning in each of the skill areas. You may use some or all of them as they are appropriate for your students.

The Assessment Tool Progress Report, as well as the practice exercises and Skinny Books, are reproducible. The teaching material offers suggestions for record keeping and can be especially helpful for student portfolios.

The student activities and practices for each skill are graduated in levels of difficulty. You can choose appropriate practices based on the ability level of each student. The progression from easier to more difficult allows each student initial success in working with the material. Clear and understandable directions are provided for student practices. For some practices, when necessary, special teaching instructions are provided.

Some Suggestions for Use

Phonics: Skills and Strategies in a Balanced Reading Program can be used in various settings and with a variety of students, regardless of the type of program you are currently using. It is particularly effective in a balanced reading program (see "What Is a Balanced Reading Program?" on page 8).

I encourage you to continuously assess your children's reading behavior. You can gain information about your students' reading behavior using observation and student portfolios, as well as, when appropriate, informal and formal diagnostic measures. You then can use this data to either reinforce, supplement, enrich, or develop skill and strategy areas.

You, the teachers, are the decision makers. You must determine, based on developmental levels of the children, the amount of instruction you need to present to your students.

What Is a Balanced Reading Program?

A balanced reading program is one in which the best of whole-language practices and a sequential development of skills are fully integrated. In such a program, teachers and parents integrate various aspects of the best of the whole-language movement with different programs to achieve a balanced, eclectic approach that is practical.

In a balanced reading program, the emphasis is on helping students improve their higher-order thinking skills as well as gain needed comprehension and word recognition skills and strategies. In such a program, teachers also nurture a love of books in their students to help them become lifelong readers.

What Is the Role of the Teacher in a Balanced Reading Program?

Teachers are the key to the success of any program. Good teachers are aware of the individual differences of students in their classrooms, the interrelatedness of reading with the other language arts, and they understand their role in the teaching of reading.

In a balanced reading program, you, the teacher, are the key decision-maker. You determine which materials, practices, skills, and strategies to use based on the individual differences of your students. In a balanced reading program, teachers use trade books, children's writings, newspapers, textbooks, and all other appropriate materials as springboards for children's listening, speaking, reading, writing, and viewing.

Instructional Strategies to Help Children Build Their Word Recognition Ability

The emphasis in *Phonics: Skills and Strategies in a Balanced Reading Program* is on providing direct instruction to the children. *Direct instruction* is instruction guided by a teacher who uses various strategies or techniques to help children become effective readers. There are a number of strategies you can use to teach reading directly. The strategies that you use should not be affected by the kinds of materials you use. In other words, one teacher may use only trade books in his or her class, while another might use a basal reader. Both teachers can employ similar strategies to help students gain needed concepts. As stated previously, this text advocates a mix of materials, beliefs, and strategies.

Interactive Instruction

In interactive instruction, the teacher intervenes at optimal times to improve instruction. The teacher determines when to intervene and what materials and strategies to use to achieve the desired learning for the readers with whom she or he is working.

Modeling Instruction

Modeling instruction requires teachers to think out loud. That is, you verbalize your thoughts to help students "see" an appropriate strategy or reading behavior. This is an exceptionally effective strategy because it helps students gain insight into the kinds of thinking involved in all aspects of reading. Throughout this book, modeling strategies will be illustrated where applicable.

Interactive instruction combined with modeling instruction is very effective in helping students gain the skills they need to become effective strategic readers.

Beginning Reading: An Explanation

Beginning reading is a child's involvement in a formal reading program. This can begin in either kindergarten or first grade. The question is: How do children figure out the mysterious symbols? How do they go from recognizing whole words that they see—for example, on food boxes, signs, and stores—to reading running text?

It makes sense that in figuring out words, children must first recognize that the words have meaning. Children then must be able to identify these words. This series is concerned with helping children become proficient in figuring out words on the printed page using phonics.

Even though phonics is a powerful tool that helps students become more self-reliant readers, and the emphasis here is on phonics, it must be stressed that reading is a total integrative process. Phonics is but one part of word recognition, which itself is but one part of the reading program. Students usually use a combination of strategies to help them unlock words.

Word Recognition Strategies

Word recognition is essential to being able to read. In this series, word recognition is considered a two-fold process—the identification of a printed word so that the word can be pronounced, and the attachment or association of meaning to the word.

Even though, as already stated, the emphasis in this series is on phonics, the various pronunciation and word meaning strategies associated with word recognition are being presented because students usually use a combination of strategies in figuring out printed words.

Pronunciation

When we read, we are intent on getting the message and appear to do so automatically. We don't notice the individual letters, groups of letters, or even every word. If we are good readers, this is what is taking place. It isn't until we stumble on an unfamiliar word that we become aware of the individual letters that are grouped together to form a word. The reason we stopped reading is because the word we stumbled on has interfered with our getting the message. The question is: Do you remember what you did when a word interfered with your understanding of what you were reading?

There are a number of strategies that can be used to figure out how to pronounce a word as well as strategies that can be used to determine the meaning of a word. These strategies are not necessarily the same.

To better understand this process, here are a number of exercises involving nonsense and actual words.

Read the following sentence:

I don't like *cland* food.

You should have stumbled on the nonsense word *cland*. Imagine that you do not know that *cland* is a nonsense word. Let's look at the kinds of strategies we could and could not use to help us gain the pronunciation of a word independently.

Strategy 1: Phonics analysis and synthesis

Definition: *Phonics* is a decoding technique that depends on students being able to make the proper letter-sound correspondences. *Analysis* has to do with the breaking down of something into its component parts. *Synthesis* has to do with the building up of parts of something into a whole.

Analysis: Break down *cland* into the blend *cl* and the word family (phonogram) *and*. We have seen the blend *cl* in such words as *climb* and *club*. We have seen the phonogram *and* in such words as *sand* and *hand*. We therefore know the pronunciations of *cl* and *and*.

Synthesis: Blend together the *cl* and *and*.

Using this technique, we should be able to pronounce *cland* or at least gain an approximation of its pronunciation. Phonics helps us figure out unfamiliar words independently.

Strategy 2: Whole word or "look and say" method

Definition: The whole word or "look and say" method, which is also referred to as the sight method, directs a student's attention to a word and then to saying the word. The student must make an association between the oral word and the written word, and he or she shows this by actually saying the word.

For this technique to be effective, the child must look at the word while pronouncing it so that the association is made between the spoken and written word. This technique is a useful word recognition strategy that helps us learn to pronounce words, but it will not help us figure out the pronunciation of unfamiliar words independently.

Strategy 3: Ask someone to pronounce the word for you

This could be done, but it would be similar to the "look and say" method, and it would not help us to figure out the word independently.

Strategy 4: Context clues

Definition: By *context*, we mean the words surrounding a word that can shed light on its meaning. When we refer to context clues, we mean clues that are given in the form of definitions, examples, comparisons or contrasts, explanations, and so on, which help us figure out word meanings.

Using context clues is a word recognition technique, but it is not one that helps us figure out the pronunciation of words. It is one that is used for helping us gain the meaning of a word (see "Word Meaning" on page 13).

Strategy 5: Structural analysis and synthesis (word parts)

Definition: Structural analysis and structural synthesis have to do with the breaking down (analysis) and building up (synthesis) of word parts, such as prefixes, suffixes, roots (bases), and combining forms.

Structural analysis is a helpful word recognition technique that can aid in the pronunciation of words, but it will not help us figure out the pronunciation of *cland*. Because *cland* is a nonsense word, it is an unfamiliar root word.

Structural analysis is especially helpful in figuring out the pronunciation of an unfamiliar word if the word is composed of familiar word parts, such as prefixes, suffixes, and roots. This strategy is similar to phonics analysis and synthesis. As an example, let's see how we would go about figuring out how to pronounce the italicized word in the following sentence using structural analysis and synthesis.

The salesperson said that the goods were not *returnable*.

Structural analysis: break down the word into its parts to isolate the root.

re - turn - able

If we had met *re* before and if we had met *able* before, we should know how to pronounce them. After we have isolated *turn*, we may recognize it as a familiar word and know how to pronounce it.

Structural synthesis: blend together *re, turn,* and *able*.

If *turn* is not a familiar root word for us, then we could apply phonics analysis to it and after that blend it together with the prefix *re* and the suffix *able*.

Strategy 6: Look up the pronunciation in the dictionary

This is a viable method, but you may not have a dictionary handy, and by the time you look up the pronunciation of the word, you may have lost the trend of what you were reading.

Let's list those techniques that can help us figure out the pronunciation of words:

1. Phonics analysis and synthesis.
2. Whole word or "look and say."
3. Asking someone.
4. Structural analysis and synthesis.
5. Looking up the pronunciation in the dictionary.

Note that phonics is the most effective pronunciation strategy for figuring out an unfamiliar word independently.

Word Meaning

Being able to pronounce a word is important, but it does not guarantee that we will then know the meaning of the word. As previously stated, word recognition is a two-fold process—correct pronunciation and meaning. After we have pronounced a word, we need to have heard the word before and know what the word means. Obviously, the larger our stock of listening vocabulary, the better able we will be to decipher the word. If we have never heard the word before, it would not be in our listening vocabulary. Therefore, the pronunciation would not act as a stimulus and trigger an association with a word that we have stored in our memory bank. Let's look at the techniques that we can use to help unlock words that we have never encountered before.

Strategy 1: Context

By *context*, we mean the words surrounding a particular word that can help shed light on its meaning. Read the following sentence:

Even though my *trank* was rather long, I wouldn't take out one word.

From the context of the sentence, you know that the nonsense word *trank* must somehow refer to a sentence, paragraph, paper, or report of some kind. Even though you never heard the word *trank* before, the context of the sentence throws light on its meaning. You know from the word order or position of the word (syntax) that *trank* must be a noun, and words like *word* and *long* give you meaning (semantic) clues to the word itself. There are times, however, when context is not too helpful, so other strategies must be used.

Strategy 2: Structural analysis and synthesis for word meaning

Read the following sentence:

We asked the *misanthrope* to leave.

From the position of the word *misanthrope* in the sentence, we know that it is a noun. However, there is not enough information to help us figure out the meaning of *misanthrope*. Structural analysis could be very useful in situations where there are insufficient context clues, and the word consists of a number of word parts.

Analysis: Break down *misanthrope* into its word parts.

Mis means either "wrong" or "hate," and *anthropo* means "humankind."

Synthesis: Put together the word parts.

It doesn't make sense to say "wrong humankind," so it must be *hate* and *humankind*. Since *misanthrope* is a noun, the meaning of *misanthrope* would have to be "hater of humankind."

Structural analysis is a powerful tool, but it is dependent on having knowledge of word parts and their meanings. If you do not have these at hand, you obviously need another strategy.

Strategy 3: Ask someone the meaning of the word

This, at times, may be the most convenient if someone is available who knows the meaning of the word.

Strategy 4: Look up the meaning in the dictionary

If you cannot figure out the word *independently* rather quickly, so that your train of thought is not completely broken, the dictionary is a valuable tool for word meanings.

Let's list those techniques that can help us figure out the meaning of words:

1. Context of a sentence.
2. Structural analysis and synthesis.
3. Asking someone.
4. Looking up the meaning in the dictionary.

Self-Correction

It is possible for context clues to help with the correction of mispronounced words that are in the listening vocabulary of the reader, but not yet in his or her reading vocabulary. Here is such an example. A student is asked to read the following sentence:

The child put on her coat.

The student reads the sentence as follows:

The *chilld* put on her coat.

The reader then self-corrects and rereads the sentence correctly. What has taken place? The first pronunciation, *chilld*, was obtained from graphic clues. As the student continued to read, the text of the sentence indicated that the mispronounced word should be *child* rather than *chilld*. Since the word *child* was in the student's listening vocabulary, he or she was able to self-correct the mispronunciation. In this case, the context clues helped the reader to correct the mispronunciation of *child*.

It is important to state that the reader would not have been able to self-correct if the word *child* had not been in his or her listening vocabulary and if he or she had not heard it correctly pronounced.

Stress to your students that phonics usually only gives an approximation of the way a word is pronounced. Often readers must rely on sentence meaning and their familiarity with the spoken word to pronounce it correctly.

Word Recognition Strategies: Some Further Remarks

It is important to be aware of the different word recognition strategies and the purpose for each so that effective teaching can take place. For example, a teacher must realize that helping a child to become proficient in phonics will not help him or her to be a good reader unless the child has developed a stock of vocabulary and has adequate concept development. A child may be able to decode all the words in a passage, but this child would not be reading unless he or she could determine the meaning of the passage. Some strategies will work better with different children. This should not, however, preclude teachers from helping children become proficient in using all the strategies and from helping children determine which strategy or strategies are best to use in a specific situation. Usually, as already stated, a combination of strategies is used.

On the following pages, you will find a graphic summary of word recognition and a sequential development of phonics skills. Use the information to develop your own step-by-step program to teach your children phonics. You will also find a diagnostic checklist of phonics skills on page 161 of this resource that you may want to include in each student's portfolio.

© Fearon Teacher Aids FE7970

Graphic Summary of Word Recognition

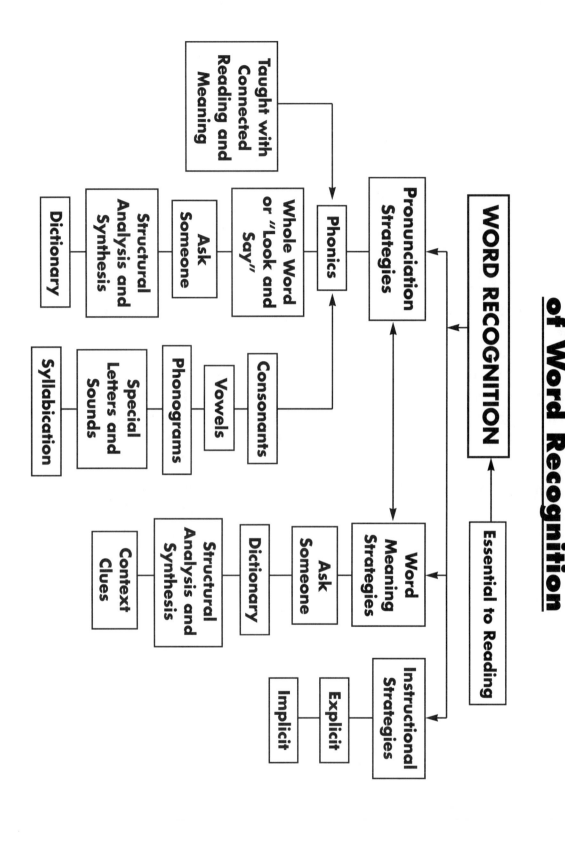

WORD RECOGNITION

Essential to Reading

Pronunciation Strategies

Word Meaning Strategies

Instructional Strategies
- Explicit
- Implicit

Pronunciation Strategies:
- Phonics
  - Taught with Connected Reading and Meaning
  - Consonants
  - Vowels
  - Phonograms
  - Special Letters and Sounds
  - Syllabication
- Whole Word or "Look and Say"
- Ask Someone
- Structural Analysis and Synthesis
- Dictionary

Word Meaning Strategies:
- Ask Someone
- Dictionary
- Structural Analysis and Synthesis
- Context Clues

A Developmental Sequence of Phonics

Although the teaching of phonics will vary according to the needs of the students, in a developmental sequence, certain skills usually should be achieved before others. So that teachers can properly diagnose the needs of their students in phonics, teachers must be proficient in this area and know the various steps involved. First, the child usually learns a few sight words. Then, when the child learns that some words look alike and/or sound alike, the mastering of phonics word attack skills has begun. This task is not a simple one.

The following is an outline of the developmental sequence of phonics instruction, which is covered in the four-level phonics series.

1. Auditory discrimination
2. Visual discrimination
3. Consonants
   a. Initial consonants
   b. Final consonants
   c. Consonant blends (clusters) (*bl, st, str*)
   d. Initial consonant blends (clusters); final consonant blends (clusters)
   e. Initial consonant digraphs (*th, ch, sh*)
   f. Final consonant digraphs (*ng, gh*)
   g. Silent consonants (*kn, pn, wr*)
4. Vowel sounds
   a. Long vowel sounds
   b. Short vowel sounds
   c. Effect of final *e* on vowel
   d. Double vowels
      1) Digraphs
      2) Diphthongs
   e. Vowel controlled by *r*
5. Special letters and sounds
6. Word families (phonograms)
7. Syllabication
   a. Meaning of syllable
   b. Generalizations

1) Double consonant—vowel consonant/consonant vowel (vc/cv)

2) Vowel-consonant-vowel (v/cv)

3) Consonant with special *le* at end of syllable (vc/cle or v/cle)

c. Syllable phonics

d. Accent

Phonics Instruction: An Explanation

The Phonics: Skills and Strategies in a Balanced Reading Program series is based on the premise that phonics instruction in the early grades is important; however, it must be taught in conjunction with meaning. The emphasis in this series is not on the stating of generalizations or rules but on children being able to internalize the generalizations or rules so that they can become proficient readers as quickly as possible.

Special Note

In phonics, the term *generalization* is preferred to the term *rule* because the latter is a more prescriptive term and implies great consistency. In working with children, however, the term *rule* is easier for them to use and understand than *generalization*. The terms are used interchangeably in this book and series.

Teaching Strategies

The two teaching strategies that are usually used in teaching phonics follow:

Explicit Phonics Instruction

In explicit phonics instruction, each sound associated with a letter in the word is pronounced in isolation and then blended together. The teacher shows the children the word *bat*, points to the letter *b*, and says that it stands for the sound *buh*. The teacher then points to the letter *a* in the word *bat* and says it stands for the sound *ah*, then points to the letter *t* and says it stands for the sound *tuh*. The children are then helped to blend the sounds *buh ah tuh* together to get *bat*.

A major problem with this method is that it is difficult to produce pure speech sounds in isolation.

Implicit Phonics Instruction

In implicit phonics instruction, the teachers do not present sounds associated with letters in isolation. The teacher states a number of words beginning with the same initial consonant. For example, the teacher asks the children to listen to the words *ball, baby,* and *book.* The teacher also writes these words on the chalkboard. The teacher tells the children that the letter *b* stands for the sound at the beginning of the words *ball, baby,* and *book.* They all have the same beginning letter *b.* They all start with the same sound. The teacher then gives more words that begin with the letter *b* and asks students to state some other words that begin like *big* or with the letter *b.*

Teachers often use a combination of both explicit and implicit phonics instruction. The important thing to remember is that any method that helps children unlock words as quickly as possible should be used. Phonics gives children the power and independence to pronounce unfamiliar words.

It is also very important to note again that phonics often does not give the exact pronunciation of a word, especially of multisyllabic words. Phonics usually gives only an approximation of the pronunciation of a word. However, if the word is in the children's listening experience, they will be able to figure out the correct pronunciation, especially if they also employ other word recognition skills and strategies.

Two sample lessons plans follow. You may wish to use these as springboards to develop other lesson plans.

Sample Lesson Plan I

Objectives

1. The children will be able to identify differences in the sounds and tones of various musical instruments.

2. The children will be able to describe the sounds of various instruments and use their imaginations to state what the musical sounds make them think of.

3. The children will be able to write a title and a short story for one of the musical selections.

Preliminary Preparation

❑ Make up a bulletin board entitled "Musical Sounds." Place pictures on the bulletin board of famous musicians playing their instruments.

❑ Have available a tape player and the recordings "Instruments of the Orchestra" and "Bear Dance" from *Hungarian Sketches* by Bela Bartok.

❑ Write the following words and phrases on the board:
brass instruments, trumpet, French horn, trombone, tuba

❑ If possible, provide real instruments for the students to use. You may be able to borrow these from the music department or ask a music teacher to bring the instruments in and demonstrate the unique sounds of each for your students.

Introduction

"We've been working with various musical instruments because many of you said that you would like to learn more about them. What are the instruments that we decided to work with first? Yes, they are called *brass instruments*. Can someone find those words on the board for me? Good. Tell me the names of the brass instruments that we have already worked with. Yes. Can someone find these words on the board and then point out the instrument on the bulletin board? Good.

"Today, I brought some music for you to listen to. The music has some new brass instruments in it. We will be working with these today. See if you can hear the new instruments. Close your eyes and allow your imaginations to roam. Try to image what is happening as you listen to the music. Listen carefully to see whether you can tell which instrument is being used."

Play "Bear Dance" from *Hungarian Sketches* by Bela Bartok.

Development

After the children listen to the recording, ask them what they thought of as they listened to the music. What kinds of sounds did they hear? Did the sounds remind them of anything or anyone?

Ask children to give you examples of the kinds of thing the music reminded them of. Some of the children's suggestions may be large clumsy animals, giants or monsters, big machines, and so on. Write children's ideas on the board. Then ask children what it was in the music that made them think of these things. Children may mention very loud noises, fast speed, tones repeated over and over, or a lot of excitement in the music. Ask children what the large, clumsy animals might be doing that the music reminds them of. They might say such things as *chasing, running, dancing,* and *rushing.*

Ask the children if they recognize any of the brass instruments they learned about the other day. Did they hear any new sounds? Invite children to state words that describe some of the new sounds they heard in the music, for example, they may suggest words like:

deep   sad
low   funny
harsh   loud
gloomy

Explain to the children that these sounds were made by two instruments that they will be learning about today. They are the trombone and the tuba. Point to those words on the board. Then tell children, "This recording has the sounds of the trombone and the tuba. First we will listen to the trombone (point to the picture). It goes up and down the scale to show you how high and how low it can go." Play the part in "Instruments of the Orchestra" that features the trombone.

"Next is the tuba (point to the picture)." Play the selection, and then turn off the music. Ask the children, "What two new instruments did we listen to today? Show us the words on the board. Can anyone point out the pictures of those instruments on the board. Good."

"Why do you think these instruments were used to represent a dancing bear?" Children may suggest:

A bear is clumsy.
He makes low, loud noises.
It sounds like a growl.

Play "Bear Dance" once more. Say to the children, "Let's play the music once more. Listen closely and see if you hear the trombone and the tuba. Hold up your left hand if you hear the trombone. Hold up your right hand if you hear the tuba."

If time permits, divide the group into four teams. Challenge each team to come up with a title for the music they just heard. Then children can write a short story telling what they think is happening during the music. Invite each team to share their title and story with the rest of the group. Then tell the children the name of the musical selection. Encourage children to discuss whether they think the actual title of the piece fits the selection.

Summary
"What have we done today?" Help children pull the main points of the lesson together.

Forward Look
"Tomorrow we will listen to a musical piece that has all four of the brass instruments we have learned about. (The musical piece is called "Circus Music.")

Sample Lesson Plan II

This review lesson is for highly able children. Teachers should take into account the developmental levels of their children when presenting this lesson.

Objectives

1. The children will be able to define the word *syllable* correctly.

2. The children will be able to determine which is done first—syllabication or phonics analysis.

3. The children will be able to state the rules of syllabication.

Preliminary Preparation

Display the following nonsense words:

slattem	paton	braitle
plamtem	crono	lastle
tropson	disat	croble

Introduction

"Today let's review the syllabication rules we have been working with. There are a number of two-syllable nonsense words on the board. How many of them can you pronounce? In order to be able to pronounce words with more than one syllable properly, what do you have to know? Do you syllabicate first, or do you put in vowel rules first? Let's see if we can apply what we've learned to the words on the board."

Development

"Who can tell me what they think we should do? Why don't you experiment first on your own." After a while, ask for volunteers to pronounce the words on the board. After each word is pronounced, ask one student to tell how he or she syllabicated the first word. Then ask the other children if they agree with the syllabication. After each word, tell the children the correct way to syllabicate and pronounce that word.

"Let's review the definition of a syllable. Can anyone tell me? Good. A syllable is a vowel or a group of letters with one vowel sound. Do you know why I used nonsense words in this lesson? Right, so that you would not be influenced by words that you know. More importantly, by using nonsense words, we can see that all syllabication rules apply, without exception."

The teacher reminds students that phonics help them pronounce words only. They still have to know what the words mean. The teacher also tells them that phonics usually only gives them an approximation of the words' pronunciation. This is especially true in words of more than one syllable. However, when we use nonsense words, as we just said, the rules always apply.

Next, ask students if they can come up with the syllabication rules that they have already learned by looking at the nonsense words that have been syllabicated. Students should come up with the three syllabication rules, which can then be listed on the board next to the nonsense syllables.

Syllabication rules

slat / tem	Vowel consonant/consonant vowel
plam / tem	(vc/cv)—divided between
trop / son	two consonants.
pa / ton	Vowel/consonant vowel
cro / no	(v/cv)—consonant goes with the
di / sat	second vowel.
brai / tle	Special consonant *le* rule—consonant
las / tle	goes with *le* to form a syllable.
cro / ble	

Ask children what they did in order to be able to pronounce the nonsense words with more than one syllable. Did they apply the vowel rule first or the syllabication rule?

Tell students that you will answer the question after you model for them what you did. Put two more examples on the board: *rommo* and *romo*. Syllabicate the two nonsense words—rom / mo and ro / mo. Then say, "As *rom* ends in a consonant, it is a closed syllable, and therefore the *o* is usually short. As *ro* ends in a vowel, it is an open syllable, and therefore the *o* is usually long."

Go back to the original question. "To pronounce a word with more than one syllable, I syllabicate first, because I do not know what the sound of the vowel will be until after I have syllabicated."

Next, give a few more examples to make sure the children understand this concept. Now ask children for examples when they should not syllabicate first.

Put the following nonsense words on the board: *depe, tope, nais, neep, noin, sloy, slog, wot, wo,* and *ta.* Ask students to tell you why they would not syllabicate these words first. Ask what *depe* and *tope* have in common. Students will note that these are both one-syllable words with the silent "e" rule. The silent "e" rule states that in words or syllables containing two vowels that are separated by a consonant, one of which is the final *e,* the first vowel is usually long and the final *e* is silent.

In the nonsense words *neep* and *nais,* the vowel combinations *ee* and *ai* are vowel digraphs. A vowel digraph is a vowel combination making one vowel sound. The nonsense words *neep* and *nais* are one-syllable words containing vowel digraphs, whereby the first vowel is usually long and the second is silent.

In the nonsense words *noin* and *sloy*, the vowel combinations are diphthongs. The nonsense words *noin* and *sloy* are one syllable words, so they, too, are not syllabicated.

In the nonsense words *slog* and *wot*, we note that both words have one vowel and each end in a consonant. Usually, the vowel is short. These two nonsense words are closed-syllable words so they are not syllabicated.

The nonsense words *wo* and *ta* both have one vowel, and both end in a vowel. The vowel is usually long. These are also one-syllable words and, therefore, are not syllabicated.

Summary

"What have we done today?" Help children pull the main points of the lesson together. Have children state the syllabication and vowel rules. Ask children when they would syllabicate first. Then invite a number of children to come to the board and make up nonsense words for the other children to syllabicate.

Forward Look

"Tomorrow we will be working with accenting. In order to pronounce two or more syllables properly, it will help to know something about accent marks."

Phonemic Awareness: A Special Note

Phonemic awareness, which is also referred to as *phoneme awareness*, is the ability to recognize that a spoken word is made up of a sequence of individual sounds. For example, in the word *hat*, the children should be able to recognize that the first sound is /h/, the second is /a/, and the last is /t/. Unless children are aware that words consist of individual sounds, they will have difficulty in decoding. Without phonemic awareness, children will not be able to discriminate between or among various sound symbols, which is an essential first step in phonics.

Teachers can help children gain phonemic awareness by presenting them with a word and then stressing an individual sound in the word. The children are asked to repeat the sound after the teacher produces it. For example, in the word *hat*, the teacher first says (/hhhat/). Note that it is only the first sound in the word that is stressed by holding it longer. The other sounds are produced as usual. The teacher does the same for all the sounds in the word; that is, next the teacher emphasizes the second sound by saying (/*haaat*/), and emphasizes the last sound by saying (/*hattt*/).

Some educators refer to those skills associated with auditory discrimination as phoneme or phonemic awareness. In this series, phonemic awareness is looked upon as an important skill that all children need in order to work with phonics. It, however, is a precursor to auditory discrimination, which itself is a precursor to phonics. Regardless as to what labels are used to refer to these important skills, children usually proceed from sound-letter correspondences to letter-sound correspondences (phonics).

This book deals with three skills that are important in order to work with phonics—special letters and sounds, syllabication, and word families (phonograms). On the following pages, you will find a review section containing a diagnostic checklist of the skills students met in the levels 2 and 3 phonics book in this series.

Phonics III Review: Skills Checklist Diagnostic Assessment

Student's Name _____

Grade _____

Teacher _____

Word Recognition Skills	yes	no	sometimes
1. The student uses a. context clues			
b. picture clues			
2. The student asks someone to state the words.			
3. The student uses the dictionary to try to unlock unknown words.			
4. The student uses phonics analysis by recognizing a. consonants			
1) single consonants: initial, final			
2) consonants blends (clusters) (*br, sl, cl, st*)			
3) consonant digraphs (*th, sh, ph, ch*)			
4) silent consonants (*kn, wr, pn*)			
b. vowels			
1) short vowels (*cot, can, get*)			
2) long vowels (*go, we, no*)			
3) final silent "*e*" (*bake, tale, role*)			

4) vowel digraphs (*ea, oa, ee, ai*)			
5) diphthongs (*oi, oy*)			
c. word families (*an, at, et, un, all, ake, ag, am, ain, ame, ay, en, ick*)			

Skill 1:
Special Letters and Sounds

Explanation

There are some letters and sounds that are exceptions to many of the generalizations or rules covered in levels 1–3 of the phonics series. These letters and sounds have their own sets of rules.

The Letter Y

The letter *y* is used as both a consonant and a vowel. When the letter *y* is used as a consonant, it is at the beginning of a word or syllable. Some examples are the words *yes, yet, your, you, young, year, canyon,* and *graveyard.* When the letter *y* acts as a vowel, it represents the short *i* sound, the long *i* sound, or the long *e* sound. The letter *y* usually represents the short *i* sound when *y* is in the middle of a word or syllable that has no vowel letter, like *hymn, gym, synonym,* and *cymbal.* The letter *y* usually represents the long *i* sound when it is at the end of a single-syllable word that has no vowel, as in such words as *by, try, sky, why, dry, fly,* and *my.* The letter *y* usually represents the long *e* sound when it is at the end of multisyllabic words, such as *baby, candy, silly, daddy, pretty, family,* and *crafty.*

Teaching Strategies in Action

The teaching of the letter *y* is best done when children have met words or will meet upcoming words with this letter in various positions within the words. The children should have already worked with long and short vowel sounds and, of course, know the difference between consonant and vowel letters.

Teachers must decide, based on the individual differences of the students, whether to present separate lessons on the various sounds of *y* based on its position in a word. It is probably a good idea to present the various sounds of *y* separately and space the lessons to give children time to practice what they have learned.

It is recommended that you present children first with *y* as a consonant and as the final letter in a one-syllable word, such as *my* that has no vowel.

After children have mastered the sound of *y* in words, such as *my* and *try;* then you should proceed to the sound of *y* at the end of two-syllable words, such as *pretty* and *tidy.* After children have worked with *y* in words, such as *pretty* and *tidy,* you should present children with words, such as *gym* and *hymn* in which *y* is in the middle of a word that has no vowels.

The *y* in multisyllabic words, such as *synonym* and *cymbal* are more difficult for children. The generalization is that when *y* is in the middle of a word or syllable that has no vowels the *y* sounds like the short *i* in *Tim.*

Give students a list of one-syllable words that end in the letter *y*, a list of two-syllable words that end in *y*, a list of words in which the letter *y* is in the center of each word, and a list of words in which the *y* is at the beginning of the word. Using an inductive technique, have the students look carefully at the four sets of words and try to discern the differences among them.

Sample Practice

Here is a sample practice you can use with your students.

Directions: Listen carefully. I will state the four words on the chalkboard that all have the letter *y*. Tell me how the *y* sounds in the four words.

yet	fry
gym	tidy

After a discussion of how the sounds that the letter *y* stands for change based on the position in a word, put more words containing *y* on the chalkboard and ask for volunteers to pronounce the words.

Help your students understand that the sound of *y* changes based on where the letter is in each word.

Modeling Strategy

Here is how one teacher models for her students how to pronounce the words and the various sounds that the letter *y* stands for. First, she says: "I know that the letter *y* has different sounds based on where it is in the word. I want to show you all the different sounds it can have, even though we will be working separately with the different *y* sounds." Then the teacher puts the following words on the chalkboard:

pry	silly
yet	gym

Next, she says and does the following:

"I know that when the letter *y* is at the beginning of a word, it is a consonant and sounds like the beginning of the word *year*. I also know that the word *yet* rhymes with the word *set*. Therefore, I can pronounce *yet*. The other words have the letter *y* at the end or middle of the words. I know that when *y* is at the end of a word or syllable, it stands for a vowel. I've also learned that when *y* is at the end of a one-syllable word that has no vowels, it sounds like long *i*. Therefore, the word spelled *p r y* probably has the long *i* sound at the end of it, so I can now pronounce *pry*. As for the next word, spelled *s i l l y*, I know that when *y* is at the end of two-syllable words and the second syllable has no vowel, the *y* sounds like the long *e*. I know, too, that *s i l l* rhymes with *pill*. Now I can pronounce the word *silly*. The last word, spelled *g y m*, has a *y* in the middle of it and there are no vowels in the word. I know that when *y* is in the middle of a word or syllable, it acts as a vowel and sounds like the short *i* as in *Tim*. Therefore, I can now pronounce the word *gym*. Do not worry we will have separate lessons on the different sounds of *y*.

The Letters C and G

Some words beginning with the letter *c* or the letter *g* can cause problems for students because the letters *c* and *g* each stand for both a soft and hard sound.

The letter *g* in the words *gym, George, gentle,* and *generation* stands for a soft *g* sound. A soft *g* sounds like the letter *j* in *Jack, jail,* and *justice*. The initial letter *g* in *go, get, gain, gone,* and *goat* stands for a hard *g* sound. Note that the letter *g* sounds either like the beginning sound of *j* as in *jail* or *g* as in *gentle*.

The beginning letter *c* in the words *cease, cent, center, censor, census,* and *cite* stands for a soft *c* sound. A soft *c* sounds like the letter *s* in the words *so, sew, same, sign,* and *Sam*. The initial letter *c* in *cat, cook, cake, can,* and *cold* stands for a hard *c* sound. A hard *c* sounds like *k* in the words *key, keep, king, kite,* and *kettle*. Note that the letter *c* sounds either like the beginning sound of *s* as in *sing* or *k* as in *king*.

Teaching Strategies in Action

The teaching of the letters *c* and *g* are best done when students have a good command of most of the phonics generalizations. Teachers must decide, based on the individual differences of the students, whether to present separate lessons on the concept of the soft and hard *c* and *g* sounds. It's probably a good idea to present the *c* and *g* sounds separately and space the lessons to give children time to practice what they have learned.

Students have probably met many words that begin with *c* and *g* or that have the letters *c* or *g* in the word. The pronunciations may have confused children because the pronunciation of the words vary based on what letters follow the *c* or *g*. There are numerous exceptions to the generalization for pronouncing words that have *c* or *g* in them. Therefore, teachers should stress that students check whether the word they are pronouncing makes sense in the context of what they are reading. Teachers should also suggest strongly that students who are unsure of a word should ask someone or look it up in the dictionary. In addition, teachers should pronounce any words with which children are having difficulty and present a lesson that helps students gain some insight into how to pronounce words with *c* or *g*. Teachers might also consider presenting a lesson on the sounds represented by *g* first because the letter *g* does have a characteristic sound of its own.

Sample Practice

Here is a sample practice you can use with your students.

Directions: Listen carefully. I will pronounce two words that begin with the letter *g*. Tell me if you hear any differences between them.

go   genius

She asks the students what they heard. She then states two more words:

give   gentle

Again she asks about the differences between the two words. The teacher puts the words on the chalkboard and keeps adding new words while at the same time pronouncing them.

The teacher and the students discuss the different sounds that the letter *g* stands for. "The letter *g* has a characteristic sound of its own when it doesn't have the vowel *e* following it. If the vowel *e* follows *g* in a word or syllable, then the *g* usually represents a soft *g* sound, like the *j* in *jam*."

The teacher does the same for the letter *c*; however, she helps students recognize that the letter *c* does not have its own characteristic sound. It either has the hard *c* sound like the letter *k* in *kite* or the soft *c* sound like the letter *s* in *soft*.

Modeling Strategy

Here is how this teacher models the concept of hard and soft *g* sounds for her students. The teacher puts two lists of words on the board. The first list contains words with the hard *g* sound and the second list contains words with the soft *g* sound. She pronounces all the words for the students. She then says, "Let me see if I can figure out any differences between the two lists." The words on the chalkboard are as follows:

go	gentle
gain	gems
give	genius
goat	general

She says "I notice that when I say the words *go, gain, give,* and *goat*, I hear the hard *g* sound. In the words *gentle, gems, genius,* and *general*, the words begin like the letter *j* in *Jack*. I'll put more words on the board and pronounce these as well. I want to see if I can notice a pattern in the words."

gold	George
gave	generous
gone	germ

"When I look at all the words that have a soft *g* sound like the *j* in *Jack*, I notice that they all have the vowel *e* following the letter *g*. It looks as though the *e* following the *g* makes the sound represented by *g* a soft sound. I know that there are exceptions to this rule. For example, in the word *get*, the *g* has the hard *g* sound. However, it does work for so many words that it's a good rule to know."

The Letter Q

The letter *q* is always followed by the letter *u* in the English language. The *qu* combination represents either one speech sound or a blend of two sounds. At the beginning of a word, *qu* almost always represents a blend of two sounds—*k* and *w*. Some examples are the words *quick*, *queen*, *quilt*, *queer*, *quack*, and *quiet*. When *qu* appears at the end of a word, in the *que* combination, it represents one sound—*k* as in *kite*. Some examples are the words *antique*, *unique*, and *clique*.

Teaching Strategies in Action

The teaching of the *qu* combination and the blend *kw* that it represents is best done when students have a good command of most of the phonics generalizations and are finding words with the *qu* combination in their reading. Also, since there are not as many words in the English language with the *que* combination as the *qu* combination, teachers should teach the *qu* combination first, even though the former represents a blend and the latter represents one consonant sound.

Sample Practice
Here is a sample practice you can use with your students.

Directions: Look carefully at the following words on the board.

quick	quilt
quiet	queen

After pronouncing the words, she asks, "What do you notice about the words? Good. They all begin with *qu* and they all sound like the beginning blend *kw*."

Modeling Strategy
The teacher puts a number of words with the *qu* combination on the chalkboard.

quiet	quart
quick	quack

queen	quiz
quilt	quit

She then says, "Let me see. All the words begin with *qu*, and they all begin with the sound of *kw*. I guess whenever I see a word beginning with *qu*, I should pronounce it like the blend *kw*. I would like to try this on some other words that have another letter in front of the *qu*, such as the following:

equal	square
squash	squirrel
squeak	squish

"Yes, these words also pronounce the letters *qu* as *kw*. Now, I'd like to see if this is also true of words that have *qu* in the middle of them. I'll pronounce each word and see if I hear the *kw* blend."

earthquake	frequent
inquire	sequence

"Yes, these words also pronounce the *qu* as *kw*. I guess this is a good rule to know.

R-Controlled Vowels

A vowel followed by the letter *r* in the same syllable is controlled by the *r*. As a result, the preceding vowel does not have its usual vowel sound. Some examples of *r*-controlled vowels are in the words *car, fir, fur, hurt, porch,* and *chart*. If a vowel is followed by the letter *r*, but the *r* begins another syllable, the vowel is <u>not</u> influenced by the *r*, for example, the words *siren, erode,* and *direct*.

Teaching Strategies in Action

A good time to teach about *r*-controlled vowels is after students have a good command of long and short vowel sounds and when students are meeting many words that have *r*-controlled vowels.

Modeling Strategy

The teacher puts two columns of words containing the letter *r* on the chalkboard. She tells her students that she will "think aloud" for them to help them recognize the differences between the two lists and how these differences usually affect the pronunciation of words that have the letter *r* in them. Here is the list of words:

car	rot
fur	roll
sir	siren

chart   enrich

pardon   enroll

The teacher says, "I will pronounce each word first to determine if I hear any differences. I notice that when a word or syllable has a vowel before the r, as in the first list, the r changes the sound of the vowel so that it is neither long nor short. If, however, the r begins a word or syllable, as it does in the second list, the r does not affect the vowel.

The Schwa (ə)

The schwa sound is symbolized by an upside down e (ə) in the phonetic (speech) alphabet. The schwa sound frequently appears in the unstressed (unaccented) syllables of words with more than one syllable. The schwa, which usually sounds like the short u in the word *but*, or the a in the word *sofa*, is represented by a number of different vowels. Some examples are the words:

P*o*lice (Pə•lēs)

d*i*vide (də•vīdȩ)

rob*u*st (rō •bəst)

Rom*a*n (Rō • mən)

In these examples, the italicized vowels represent the schwa sound. Although the spelling of the unstressed syllable in each word is different, the sound remains the same for the different vowels. The schwa, a neutral vowel, is also called an *indeterminate vowel*.

Special Notes

The pronunciations presented here are from *Webster's New Collegiate Dictionary*, but it should not be inferred that these are the only pronunciations for these words. Pronunciations may vary from dictionary to dictionary and from region to region. Different dictionaries also vary as to their use of the schwa sound.

Some language arts and reading books do not have special lessons dedicated to the schwa because the concept can be confusing for children. The schwa is an advanced concept that, if it is introduced, is presented in the upper primary grades or intermediate grades when students are working with syllabication generalizations, in particular, the "special *le*" syllabication generalization (see "Skill 2: Syllabication" for information on the "special *le*" syllabication generalization and the schwa).

Learning Objectives

❑ To be able to recognize and correctly choose one-syllable words that have no vowels and end in *y* that have the long *i* sound (practices 1–2).

❑ To be able to recognize and correctly choose words that end in *y* that have the long *e* sound (practices 3–4).

❑ To be able to differentiate between words that end in *y* that sound like long *e* and long *i* (practices 5–9).

❑ To be able to differentiate between the hard and soft *c* sounds (practices 10–14).

❑ To be able to differentiate between the hard and soft *g* sounds (practices 15–19).

❑ To be able to recognize and correctly choose words that begin with *qu* and sound like *kw* (practices 20–21).

❑ To be able to recognize and correctly choose words with *r*-controlled vowels. (practice 22).

Directions for Student Practices

Use the student practices (pages 38–59) to help your children acquire, reinforce, and review special letters and sounds. Pick and choose the practices based on the needs and developmental levels of your students. Answers for the student practice pages are on pages 162–163.

IMPORTANT:

When working with special letter and sounds, you should do the practices with the children. Have the children listen carefully as you read the directions to them. You may need to repeat the directions for your students as you do the practices. This, of course, depends on the individual differences of the students.

Extensions

Spelling and the "C" Sound

When presenting the letter *c* and the sounds that it represents, correlate this activity with spelling. Tell students that you notice that some of the words in their writing are misspelled, such as *icy, noticing, picnicking,*

© Fearon Teacher Aids FE7970

panicky, policing, and so on. Explain that there is a rule that could help them spell lots of words that end in *c* and *ce*. First, put a number of words on the board that end in *c*. Then add an ending to the word beginning with *i, e,* or *y*. Pronounce each word, and then ask them to come up with the rule.

mimic	mimicker
traffic	trafficking
frolic	frolicking
panic	panicky
picnic	picnicking

Next, do the same for words ending in *ce*. Put a number of words on the board that end in *ce*. Then add an ending to each word beginning with *i* or *y*. Pronounce each word then ask the children to come up with the rule.

notice	noticing
practice	practicing
police	policing
ice	icy
lace	lacy

Help students figure out the rule that states that in order to retain the hard *c* sound before adding an ending beginning with *i, e,* or *y*, they must add the letter *k* before the ending.

Help students recognize that words end in *ce* have a soft *c* sound. In words that have a soft *c* sound that end in *e*, drop the *e* before adding an ending beginning with *i* or *y* to retain their soft *c* sound. Finally, have children generate other words using this rule.

The Queen's Quiet Quest

Invite children to make up a class story, using as many *q* words as they can think of. Write the children's story on chart paper, and then invite children to illustrate each page. Display the finished story along one wall of your room.

Hard and Soft "C" Relay

On the board have two headings. One for hard *c* sound words and one for soft *c* sound words. Divide the class into two teams of children. Have first child write a word under either heading. Children alternate writing words under the correct heading. Play continues until someone misses. Children can collaborate to generate words.

Student's Name _____

Assessment Tool Progress Report

Progress

Improvement

Comments

© Fearon Teacher Aids FE7970
Reproducible

Name _____

Practice 1

Directions: Put a line under all the words in which the letter **y** sounds like long **i**, as the **i** in **bike**.

<u>dry</u>   happy   sorry   candy   dreary

tray   jay   <u>why</u>   daddy   family

<u>my</u>   <u>fry</u>   tidy   <u>shy</u>   sly

stormy   baby   <u>cry</u>   say   pretty

Name _____

Practice 2

Directions: Fill in the word that best fits the sentence.

1. Maya was looking for a towel to _____dry_____ her wet hair.
   (shy (dry))

2. The _____shy_____ child didn't want to greet the new
   neighbors. ((shy) cry)

3. The unhappy child said she would _____cry_____ if her parents
   made her go to the party alone. (shy (cry))

4. Lisa said that she would _____try_____ out for the play.
   (cry try)

5. _____Why_____ don't you want to go to the party?
   (Try (Why))

6. A _____fly_____ was buzzing around the food. (fry (fly))

7. _____my_____ brother is big for his age. ((My) Shy)

8. I tried to _____pry_____ open the jar cover. (play (pry))

Name _____

Practice 3

Directions: Put a line under all the words in which the letter **y** sounds like long **e**, as the **e** in **seen**.

pretty	say	salty	sly	cherry
dirty	try	muddy	hymn	gym
sorry	gray	merry	daddy	why
shy	by	berry	bury	penny

Name _____

Practice 4

Directions: Fill in the word that best fits the sentence.

1. My friend says that she likes to eat one __berry__ at a time. (bury (berry))

2. When my pet died, we had to __bury__ it. (berry (bury))

3. The __happy__ dog wagged its tail for us. (hurry (happy))

4. The large bunny's ears were white and __fluffy__. ((fluffy) tiny)

5. I like to drink __cherry__ soda, but my brother likes chocolate. ((cherry) cheery)

6. We went to a birthday __party__ yesterday. (sorry (party))

7. The __silly__ clown laughed and laughed. (chilly (silly))

8. My sister does not like to be in a __chilly__ room. ((chilly) silly)

© Fearon Teacher Aids FE7970
Reproducible

Name _____

Practice 5

Directions: Put a circle around all the words that end in **y** that have a long **e** sound. Put a line under all the words that end in **y** that have a long **i** sound.

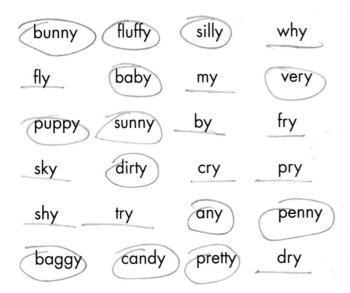

Name _____

Practice 6

Directions: Put a circle around all the words that end in **y** that have a long **e** sound. Put a line under all the words that end in **y** that have a long **i** sound. Put an X on the word if it ends in a different vowel sound.

sunny   Mary   merry   shy

sandy   candy   muddy   sleepy

pay   silly   cry   why

sky   hay   dirty   tray

try   may   puppy   bury

sorry   Andy   Molly   pray

play   pony   bray   bunny

© Fearon Teacher Aids FE7970

Name _____

Practice 7

Directions: Choose a word from the word list that names each picture.
A word may be used only once.

**baby   bunny   cherry   donkey   fly   forty   money
penny   puppy   thirty**

1.   penny

2.   cherry

3.   fly

4.   bunny

5.   baby

6. **40**   forty

7.   donkey

8.   puppy

9. **30**   thirty

10.   money

Name _____

Practice 8

Directions: Choose a word from the word list that best fits each space in the story. A word may be used only once.

~~away baby cry early easy happy lonely Molly only puppy shy silly sorry sunny very why~~

It was a hot, __sunny__ day when my best friend, Jim, came to visit
                    1

me. He used to live near me, but he moved far __away__ last year. Jim
                                                2

is __shy__. It is not __easy__ for him to make friends. Jim did not
     3   4

want to move. Before they moved away, he said that if his family moved,

he would __cry__ like a __baby__. When Jim asked his parents
          5   6

__why__ they had to move, his parents said that they, too, were
  7

__sorry__ they had to move. They knew it would be __very__
  8   9

hard on him and his sister. They, however, had to move closer to their jobs

because in the __early__ morning it took them too long to get to
                10

work. Jim's parents also said they would get a pet for him and his sister.

They did not want them to be __lonely__ when they moved.
                                11

Jim and his sister loved their new __puppy__. They named her
                                    12

__Molly__. Jim felt that the pet was the __only__ good thing
   13   14

about their move. Their pet could roll over and do __silly__ tricks. Their
                                                   15

pet made Jim and his sister laugh. Their pet made them __happy__.
                                                       16

Name _____

Practice 9

Directions: Change the underlined word in each sentence below to a word in the word list so that each sentence makes sense. A word may be used only once.

~~bunny~~ ~~dirty~~ ~~happy~~ jelly puppy ~~shy~~ ~~silly~~ sixty
~~sky~~ ~~sunny~~

1. The very <u>jumpy</u> clown made us laugh. _____silly_____

2. The <u>puppy</u> had fluffy ears and liked to eat carrots. _____bunny_____

3. Mary was so <u>sad</u> that she laughed and laughed. _____happy_____

4. <u>Friendly</u> people don't like to meet other people. _____shy_____

5. The <u>cat</u> barked. _____puppy_____

6. The <u>grass</u> is blue. _____sky_____

7. When the sun is out, it is a <u>rainy</u> day. _____sunny_____

8. After rolling in the mud, my socks were very <u>clean</u>. _____dirty_____

9. My grandfather is <u>six</u> years old. _____sixty_____

10. I like to have peanut butter and <u>stone</u> sandwiches. _____jelly_____

Name _____

Practice 10

Directions: Listen carefully. If the word I say has a **soft c** sound at the beginning, as in the word **cent**, put a line under it. If the word has a **hard c** sound at the beginning, as in the word **cook**, put a circle around it.

1. face

2. cement

3. cave

4. carrot

5. cake

6. candy

7. cent

8. cook

9. celery

10. cold

Name _____

Practice 11

Directions: Listen carefully. Some of the words I will say have a **soft c** sound, as in the word **mice**, and some have a **hard c** sound, as in the word **picnic**. Put a line under all the words I say that have a **soft c** sound.

1. nickel

2. nice

3. cookie

4. race

5. face

6. pack

7. pick

8. place

9. cement

10. pencil

Name _____

Practice 12

Directions: Put a circle around the pictures whose name has a **soft c** sound.

1.

2.

3.

4.

5.

6.

7.

8.

49

Name _____

Practice 13

Directions: Match each picture with the word that names it.

1.   branch

2.   cake

3.   ice

4.   carrot

5.   cat

6.   pencil

7.   ace

8.   face

Name _____

Practice 14

Directions: Fill in the blank with the word that best fits the sentence. A word may be used only once.

**cake   carrot   center   cereal   ice   lace   place   race
slice   space**

1. A _____ is good to eat and good for your eyes.

2. The _____ melted.

3. I eat _____ in the morning.

4. May I have a _____ of bread?

5. Did you bake the _____ for Mark's birthday party?

6. Will you have pretty _____ on your party dress?

7. Put the flowers in the _____ of the table.

8. Jim helped his team win the _____.

9. Did you _____ your books on your desk?

10. The rocketship went into _____.

Name _____

Practice 15

Directions: Listen carefully. If the word I say has a **soft g** sound at the beginning, as in the word **gentle**, put a line under it. If the word has a **hard g** sound at the beginning, as in the word **good**, put a circle around it.

1. gold

2. George

3. golf

4. get

5. gym

6. gone

7. goat

8. giant

9. gem

10. gown

Name _____

Practice 16

Directions: Listen carefully. Some of the words I say will have a **soft g** sound, as in the word **gentle**, and some will have a **hard g** sound, as in the word **go**. Put a line under only those words I say that have a **soft g** sound. Hint: The **soft g** sound may be anywhere in the word.

1. gym

2. get

3. go

4. giraffe

5. goat

6. gem

7. George

8. giant

9. cage

10. page

Name _____

Practice 17

Directions: Put a circle around the pictures whose name has a **soft g** sound. Put a line under the pictures that have a **hard g** sound. Hint: The **soft** or **hard g** sound may be anywhere in the word that names the picture.

1.

2.

3.

4.

5.

6.

7.

8.

Name _____

Practice 18

Directions: Match each picture with the word that names it.

1.   igloo

2.   giraffe

3.   gum

4.   rug

5.   gate

6.   dog

7.   cage

8.   goat

Name _____

Practice 19

Directions: Fill in the blank with the word that best fits the sentence. A word may be used only once.

**cage   dog   fog   game   gentle   George   get   giant
giraffe   goat**

1. The _____ was so thick, we couldn't see where we were going.

2. My team won the _____.

3. In the story, the _____ was taller than a house.

4. My brother, _____, is my best friend.

5. Why is your _____ always barking?

6. Please _____ me a drink of water.

7. Do you keep your pet snake in a _____?

8. The _____ has a very long neck.

9. My _____ eats paper.

10. Be very _____ with the little baby.

Name _____

Practice 20

Directions: Read the words in the word list. Write the word that names the picture. A word or phase may be used only once.

**carrot giraffe goat quarter queen question mark
quilt zipper**

1.  _____

2.  _____

3.  _____

4.  _____

5.  _____

6.  _____

7. _____

8. _____

57

Name _____

Practice 21

Directions: Choose a word or phrase from the word list that best fits the sentence. A word or phrase may be used only once.

**carrots   king   quack   quart   quarters   queen
question mark   quick   quiet   quilt**

1. Bunnies like to eat _____.

2. The candy bar costs three _____.

3. Please buy a _____ of milk.

4. In the fairy tale, a _____ and _____
   live in a castle.

5. A duck says, "_____!"

6. Please be _____ so he won't hear us.

7. My _____ keeps me warm at night.

8. Put a _____ at the end of a sentence that asks
   something.

9. The running child was too _____ for his mother to
   catch him.

Name _____

Practice 22

Directions: Put a line under all the words in which the letter **r** changes the vowel sound.

car	barn	trip	brick
sir	drip	ride	strain
train	shrimp	trick	wren
roll	bark	truck	star
bird	far	burn	rain

© Fearon Teacher Aids FE7970
Reproducible

Special Letters and Sounds

Skinny Book: The Tortoise and the Hare

On the following pages are reproducibles to make into a "Skinny Book." These Skinny Books are short, illustrated stories related to the presented skills. These small books are reproducible for distribution to children in classrooms or at home. The books are not only important time-savers for busy teachers but also important aids for parents who want to help their children succeed in learning to read.

Skinny Books are included in individual workbooks, which are available separately.

The Skinny Books are designed to be assembled easily to make individual Skinny Books for the children. If you do not have individual workbooks, you must first photocopy the pages you need for each child. Cut each page in half along the dotted line. Each page is numbered for ease of assembly. Place the pages in numerical order and staple the pages together along the left-hand side. Now you have a Skinny Book!

Make a copy for each child in your group. Children can color each page. You may also choose to make larger photocopies to make a Big Skinny Book for your "master copy." Or, ask student or adult volunteers to color and assemble each of the Skinny Book copies for you and keep a complete set for classroom use.

The Story

This is a fable about the Tortoise and the Hare. Have the children follow along with you as you look at and read the Skinny Book together. Discuss each of the pages.

Page 1

The Tortoise and the Hare meet.

Page 2

The Tortoise challenges the Hare to a race.

Page 3

The Hare thinks he is too fast for the Tortoise

Page 4

The Fox will be the judge.

Page 5

The race begins, with the Tortoise left far behind.

Page 6

The Hare decides to take a nap.

Page 7

The Tortoise moved ahead slowly and steadily as the Hare slept.

Page 8

The Tortoise passed the Hare as he slept.

Page 9

The Hare awoke and found that the Tortoise had won the race.

Pages 10 and 11

Words in the Skinny Book

Page 12

Study Question

Skill 2:

Syllabication

Explanation

A syllable is a vowel or a group of letters with one vowel sound. *Syllabication* is the process of breaking known and unknown multisyllabic words into single syllables. This is important in word recognition because, in order to be able to pronounce the multisyllabic word, a child must first be able to syllabicate it.

Teaching Strategies in Action

The teaching of syllabication usually takes place in the third or fourth grade. However, as has been stated throughout the phonics series, when to teach syllabication should be based on the developmental levels of your students.

In deciphering multisyllabic words, students must first analyze the word, determine the syllabic units, apply phonics analysis to the syllables, and then blend the syllables into a whole word. The vowel generalizations that students have learned beginning in first grade should be reviewed—these same generalizations will be used in the application of phonics analysis.

For multisyllabic words, the results will almost always be an *approximation* of the pronunciation. As for one-syllable words, the correct pronunciation will depend on the students' having heard the word and whether it makes sense in context. Usually students will have more success applying phonics to monosyllabic words than to multisyllabic ones because the blending of the syllables into a whole word often changes the pronunciation. (see "Accenting Words" later in this section.)

Special Notes

Before teachers present syllabication generalizations to their students, they must make sure their students understand what a syllable is and that every syllable must contain a vowel or a group of letters that stand for one vowel sound. Students should also be reminded that the letter *y* acts as a vowel in words that have no vowels, such as *fry, my,* and *gym.*

Because multisyllabic words must be syllabicated before applying phonics analysis, syllabication generalizations will be presented first. What follows are the major syllabication generalizations that are usually taught.

In phonics, the term *generalization* is preferred to the term *rule* because the latter is a more prescriptive term and implies great consistency. In working with children, however, you might want to use the term *rule* because it is easier for them to use and understand than the term *generalization*. The terms *rule* and *generalization* are used interchangeably in the phonics books.

© Fearon Teacher Aids FE7970

Syllabication Generalizations

Generalization 1

A vowel followed by two consonants and a vowel (vc/cv).

If the first vowel in a multisyllabic word is followed by two consonants and a vowel, the word is divided between the two consonants.

Sample Practice

Present students with a number of multisyllabic words that have been syllabicated that follow the vc/cv generalization:

can / dy	cham / ber
but / ter	thir / ty
com / ment	par / ty
num / ber	

Ask students to explain why they think you syllabicated the words as you did. Present more words as students derive the syllabication generalization.

Modeling Strategy

Here is how one teacher helps her students understand the vc/cv generalization in syllabication. She tells students that she will say aloud how she figures out the syllabication rule for the syllabicated words previously presented. She says, "Let me see. I notice that all the words have two consonants in the center of the word. I also see that the two consonants do not have to be the same. I see, too, that there is a vowel before and after the two consonants. It looks to me that the rule must be that you divide a word between two consonants if there is a vowel before and after the two consonants. Let me see if this works for all the words. Yes, it does. Good. Here are some words for you to try on your own."

The teacher then gives students a number of words that follow the vc/cv generalization.

Generalization 2

A vowel followed by a single consonant and a vowel (v/cv).

If the first vowel in a multisyllabic word is followed by one consonant and a vowel, the consonant usually goes with the second syllable.

Sample Practice

Present students with a number of multisyllabic words that have been syllabicated that follow the v/cv generalization:

fe / ver	ti / ger
be / gin	pi / lot
pu / pil	si / lent

Ask students to explain why they think you syllabicated the words as you did. Present more words as students derive the syllabication generalization.

Modeling Strategy

The teacher says the following, which refers to the syllabicated words previously presented. "Let me see. I notice that all the words have one consonant in the center of the word. I also see that there is a vowel before the consonant and a vowel after it. I see, too, that the consonant goes with the second vowel to form a syllable. It looks to me that the rule must be that you divide a word after the first vowel if that vowel is followed by a consonant and another vowel. Let me see if this works for all the words. Yes, it does. Good. Here are some words for you to try on your own."

The teacher then gives students a number of words that follow the v/cv generalization.

Special Note

After the students have learned the v/cv generalization, the teacher should help the students recognize that there is an exception to this generalization. If the letter *x* is between two vowels, the *x* goes with the first vowel rather than the second. For example:

ex / it	ex / ist
ex / act	ex / ile
ox / en	

Generalization 3

A vowel or consonant followed by a consonant plus *le* (v/cle) or (vc/cle).

If a consonant comes just before *le* in a word of more than one syllable, the consonant goes with the *le* to form the last syllable.

Sample Practice

Present students with a number of multisyllabic words that have been syllabicated and follow the v/cle or vc/cle generalization:

can / dle	daz / zle
sam / ple	bea / gle
an / kle	ca / ble
bun / dle	cra / dle

Ask students to explain why they think you syllabicated the words as you did. Present more words as students derive the syllabication generalization.

Modeling Strategy

The teacher says the following, which refers to the syllabicated words previously presented. "Let me see. I notice that all the words end in *le* and they all have a consonant before the *le*. I also see that the words are divided so that the consonant plus the *le* stand alone to form a syllable. I see that if there are two consonants before the *le*, only one consonant goes with the *le* to form the special *le* syllable. It looks to me that the rule must be that if a word ends in *le* preceded by a consonant, the consonant goes with the *le* to form a syllable. Let me see if this works for all the words. Yes, it does. Good. Here are some words for you to try on your own."

The teacher then gives students a number of words that follow the v/cle or vc/cle generalization.

Generalization 4

Compound words are divided between the two words.

cow / girl	girl / friend
cow / boy	boy / friend
base / ball	

Generalization 5

Prefixes and suffixes usually stand as whole units.

re / do	care / ful
un / dress	sheep / ish
re / turn	kind / ly
play / ful	

Phonics Applied to Syllabicated Words

After a word has been divided into syllables, the student must determine how to pronounce the individual syllables. It's a good idea at this time to review the major phonics generalizations with students, because the syllables' pronounciation will be determined by the phonics generalizations. Teachers should help students recognize that the purpose is to be able to pronounce the word as quickly as possible and that phonics is only a pronunciation skill. The students still need to know the meanings of the words.

Review of Phonics Generalizations

Open Syllable—contains one vowel and ends in a vowel. The vowel is usually sounded as long, as in the word *go*.

Closed Syllable—contains one vowel and ends in a consonant. The vowel is usually sounded as short, as in the word *sat*.

Vowel Digraph—two vowels that stand for one vowel sound. Examples of vowel digraphs are *ai, ee, ea, oa,* and *ay*.

Diphthong—a blend of vowel sounds beginning with the first and gliding to the second of two vowels. For example, *oi* and *oy*.

Silent "e"—two vowels separated by a consonant, one vowel being a final *e*, is a clue that the first vowel is usually long and the final *e* is silent. Some examples are the words *bake, broke,* and *bike*.

R-controlled vowel—a vowel followed by *r* in the same syllable is a clue that the vowel sound is controlled by the *r*—the vowel sound is neither long nor short. Examples are the words *car, sir, hare, pair,* and *horn*.

Application of Vowel Generalizations to Syllabication

Generalization 1—Double Consonant Generalization (vc/cv). The closed-syllable vowel generalization would apply to a syllable that contains one vowel and ends in a consonant. The vowel sound is usually short, as in the first syllable of *candy* and in both syllables of *asset*.

> căn / dy
> ăs / sĕt

Generalization 2—Vowel Consonant Vowel Generalization (v/cv). The open-syllable generalization would apply to a syllable that contains one vowel and ends in a vowel. The vowel sound is usually long, as in the first syllable of all the presented words.

> bē / gin   ō / pen
> tī / ger   dē / tour

Generalization 3—Special Consonant *le* Generalization (vc/cle) or (v/cle). If the syllable is closed, as in the first syllables of *saddle* and *candle*, then the vowel sound is usually short in the closed syllable, for it ends in a consonant and there is only one vowel in the syllable. If the syllable is open, as in the first syllables of

73

fable and *bugle*, then the vowel sound is usually long in the first syllable because the syllable ends in a vowel and there is only one vowel.

săd / dle	fā / ble
căn / dle	bū / gle

The letter combinations containing *le*, such as *ble*, *cle*, *dle*, *gle*, and *tle*, usually stand as the final syllable. This final syllable is not accented; it is always an unstressed syllable containing the schwa sound. (See information on the schwa sound on page 34.)

sim / pəl	ap / pəl
fab / bəl	bu / gəl
sad / dəl	

Special Note

A syllable in a multisyllabic word could also contain an *r*-controlled vowel (car / rot), a vowel digraph (rea / son), a diphthong (doi / ly), or follow the silent "e" rule (bro / cade). All these would influence the pronunciation of a syllable.

Accenting

Explanation

Accenting deals with stress; that is, which syllable is emphasized. The stress of a word is important because the way a word is accented will determine its meaning. Accenting therefore is especially important with homographs—words that are spelled the same but have different meanings based on their pronunciation.

For example: **ref' / use** (noun) means trash; **re / fuse'** (verb) means unwilling to accept.

Teaching Strategies in Action

Accenting is usually taught in conjunction with syllabication. Again, when this is taught should be based on the individual differences of your students.

To pronounce words of more than one syllable, students should syllabicate the word, apply phonics analysis, and then blend the syllables into one word. To blend the syllables into one word correctly, children need to know something about accenting and how accents affect vowel sounds.

Teachers should help students recognize that unaccented syllables are usually

74

softened, and if the syllable of a multisyllabic word is unstressed, it usually contains the schwa sound. However, not all unstressed syllables contain the schwa sound—dictionaries differ, so it's a good idea for students to check their dictionaries. As already stated, students should learn that syllables that contain the unstressed special *le* syllable, such as *ble, cle,* and *tle,* always contain the schwa sound.

Examples: able—a / bəl   candle—can / dəl

Introducing Accenting

The teacher places a number of two-syllable syllabicated words on the chalkboard:

pi / lot	bot / tle
a / ble	rea / son
den / tist	wi / zard
help / ful	

The teacher explains that even though students are able to syllabicate the individual words and are able to apply the proper phonics analysis, in order to pronounce the words correctly, they still must know something about accenting the words.

The teacher asks the students to listen as she pronounces each word to determine which syllable is stressed. The teacher then invites individual students to volunteer to pronounce the words and explains that the syllable that is sounded with more stress in a two-syllable word is called the *accented syllable*. The teacher explains that the accent mark (´) is used to show which syllable is stressed—that is spoken with greater intensity or loudness. This mark usually comes right after and slightly above the accented syllable. (Some dictionaries, such as *Webster's Third New International Dictionary*, have the accent mark come before the syllable that is stressed.)

The teacher further explains that the dictionary has a key to pronunciation of words and that the marks that show how to pronounce words are called *diacritical marks*. The most often used diacritical marks are the breve (˘) and the macron (¯), which students have already learned as the symbols for short and long vowel sounds. The accent (´) is also in the class of diacritical marks.

Modeling Strategy

Here is how one teacher models for her students how two-syllable words are accented. The teacher places a number of two-syllable syllabicated words on the chalkboard in which the first syllable is accented. She places another list on the board as well in which the second syllable is accented.

pi´/ lot	ap / point´
a´ / ble	sub / due´
den´ / tist	pro / ceed´
help´ / ful	pa / rade´
bot´/ tle	com / plain´
rea´ / son	as / tound´
wi´ / zard	po / lite´
jour´/ nal	pro / vide´
lo´ / cal	

The teacher reviews the syllabication and vowel generalizations and pronounces each of the words in both lists. She then says:

"I notice that all the words are two-syllable words and that in the first column, the accent is on the first syllable. I see that the second column has the accent on the second syllable. The only difference that I can see is that the second column of words has two vowels in its second syllable; whereas the first column of words only has one vowel in its second syllable. The generalization must then be that in two-syllable words, the first syllable is usually stressed, except when the second syllable contains two vowels.

Special Notes

Because dictionaries differ, it doesn't make sense to have students learn numerous accenting generalizations. The accenting generalizations dealing with two-syllable words that are presented hold true for a number of cases, so it does pay to teach these.

It's also important for students to know that when syllables are blended together, the pronunciation is usually not the same as the syllable-by-syllable pronunciation.

Learning Objectives

❑ To be able to recognize that a syllable is a vowel or a group of letters with one vowel sound. (practice 1).

❑ To be able to recognize whether a regular or nonsense word has one or two syllables when the word is said aloud (practices 2–3).

❑ To be able to determine whether a regular or nonsense word has one or two syllables (practices 4–5).

❑ To be able to syllabicate two-syllable regular and nonsense words. (practices 6–16).

❑ To be able to syllabicate and insert accent marks in two-syllable regular and nonsense words (practices 17–19).

Directions for Student Practices

Use the student practices (pages 80–98) to help your children acquire, reinforce, and review syllabication generalizations. Pick and choose the practices based on the needs and developmental levels of your students. Answers for the student practice pages are on pages 163–164.

IMPORTANT:

When working with syllabication, you should do the practices with the children. Have the children listen carefully as you read the directions to them. You may need to repeat the directions for your students as you do the practices. This will, of course, depend on the individual differences of the students.

Certain practices require the teacher to say aloud the words to students. See student practices for these words.

Extensions

Syllable Bulletin Board
Display the words "Syllables and Words" on the bulletin board. Then write the first or second syllables of many of the two-syllable words children are familiar with on the bulletin board. Invite children to write the missing syllables to add to the board.

Syllable Dictionary Game
Divide the group into teams of three or four children. Give each team three different words and then have them look up the words in different dictionaries to check if the syllabication is the same in each dictionary. Then, as a group, choose one dictionary that you will use as the "master." Combine the teams of children into two larger teams. Have each team choose two-syllable words from that dictionary to challenge the other team to syllabicate. For example, one team may choose the word *bottle*. The

other team must have one person syllabicate the word on the board. Then that team chooses a word and challenges the first team to syllabicate it. Play the game for ten minutes. The team with the most correct syllabications is the winner.

Clapping Game

Invite children to begin clapping their hands. Choose a child to say a multisyllabic word, such as *monster*. That child points to another child who then, while still clapping, must correctly syllabicate the word and come up with another word to be syllabicated that follows the same generalization. This game can be played in teams. You can decide whether the word is correctly syllabicated. Also, you may want to initiate another syllabication generalization as the game continues.

Wordsmiths

After learning about compound words, play this wordsmith game. Divide the group into teams of three or more children. Give each team a sheet of paper and a pencil. Then tell them they have five minutes to come up with as many compound words as they can think of. You may want to start them out by listing words on the board that can be made into compound words. The team with the most words at the end of the time period is the winner.

Student's Name _____

Assessment Tool Progress Report

Progress

Improvement

Comments

Name _____

Practice 1

Directions: Put a line under all the following that are syllables.

1. th	5. bl	9. shr	13. be
2. cra	6. bal	10. dr	14. fly
3. cot	7. ban	11. dol	15. sh
4. pen	8. my	12. snow	

Name _____

Practice 2

Directions: Listen carefully to the words I say. On your page, write the number 1 if it is a one-syllable word and the number 2 if it is a two-syllable word. For example, the word **book** is a one-syllable word because you hear only one vowel sound. The word **baby**, however, is a two-syllable word because you hear two vowel sounds.

1. peanut _____

2. pick _____

3. pill _____

4. pumpkin _____

5. nut _____

6. chestnut _____

7. cut _____

8. reason _____

9. dog _____

10. player _____

11. dance _____

12. dancing _____

13. drive _____

14. driver _____

15. call _____

Name _____

Practice 3

Directions: Listen carefully. I will say a nonsense word. Write the number 1 if it is a one-syllable nonsense word and the number 2 if it is a two-syllable nonsense word. For example, for the nonsense word **cro**, I would write the number one because I only hear one vowel sound. The nonsense word **crono**, however, is a two-syllable word because I hear two vowel sounds. Therefore, I would write the number two.

1. dram _____

2. dramete _____

3. foat _____

4. broat _____

5. broato _____

6. cham _____

7. choi _____

8. cratoi _____

9. che _____

10. slery _____

11. pignut _____

12. broteam _____

13. slickete _____

14. dra _____

15. drale _____

Name _____

Practice 4

Directions: Put one line under the words that have one syllable and two lines under those that have two syllables.

1. table

2. draw

3. deck

4. tired

5. parent

6. carrot

7. sign

8. fly

9. go

10. chase

11. signal

12. dress

13. down

14. dreamer

15. drown

Name _____

Practice 5

Directions: Put one line under the nonsense words that have one syllable and two lines under those that have two syllables.

1. cro   9. blim

2. crono   10. protom

3. crad   11. breteme

4. ded   12. kol

5. dramet   13. quoi

6. pli   14. poy

7. plem   15. pomle

8. drime

Name _____

Practice 6

Directions: Syllabicate the two-syllable words below by placing a slash (/) between the syllables. Remember, if a two-syllable word has a vowel-consonant-consonant-vowel pattern, divide the word between the two consonants. Note: Not all the words are two-syllable words.

1. crate

2. mirror

3. butter

4. bag

5. window

6. barber

7. brag

8. tender

9. comment

10. candy

11. splash

12. garbage

13. corner

14. pardon

15. cut

Name _____

Practice 7

Directions: Syllabicate the two-syllable words below by placing a slash (/) between the syllables. Remember, if a two-syllable word has a vowel-consonant-vowel pattern, divide the word so that the consonant goes with the second vowel. Note: Not all the words are two-syllable words.

1. reason

2. pilot

3. plate

4. car

5. tire

6. police

7. poison

8. bride

9. bowl

10. ant

11. lazy

12. baby

13. crazy

14. pull

15. favor

Name _____

Practice 8

Directions: Syllabicate the two-syllable words below by placing a slash (/) between the syllables. Remember, if a two-syllable word ends in **le** and has a consonant before the **le**, the consonant goes with the **le** to form a special **le** syllable. Note: Not all the words are two-syllable words.

1. bundle

2. cradle

3. bottle

4. saddle

5. sole

6. scale

7. mail

8. beagle

9. dazzle

10. sparkle

11. mole

12. pole

13. purple

14. slope

15. sample

© Fearon Teacher Aids FE7970
Reproducible

Name _____

Practice 9

Directions: Syllabicate the two-syllable words below.

1. pilot

2. candy

3. bracelet

4. slipper

5. bundle

6. pardon

7. pillow

8. season

9. muzzle

10. puddle

11. mirror

12. dirty

13. open

14. ankle

15. winner

Name _____

Syllabication Review Activity 1

Practice 10

Directions: Look at each word below and decide where the first syllable ends. Draw a line between the first and second syllable of the word. Write the number of the clue listed below on the line next to each word to show how you know where the first syllable ends. The first three words are done for you. Here are three clues that will help you:

1. can / dy, mit / ten—vowel followed by two consonants and a vowel.

2. o / pen, bea / con, la / dy—vowel followed by a single consonant and a vowel.

3. bu / gle, rum / ble, strug / gle—final **le** preceded by a consonant.

1. gar / bage ___1___

2. a / ble ___3___

3. pu / pil ___2___

4. handle _____

5. master _____

6. collar _____

7. pronounce _____

8. nimble _____

9. giggle _____

10. hobby _____

11. mirror _____

12. maple _____

13. beacon _____

14. eager _____

15. pepper _____

Name _____

Syllabication Review Activity 2

Practice 11

Directions: Look at each word below and decide where the first syllable ends. Draw a line between the first and second syllable of the word. Write the number of the clue listed below on the line next to each word to show how you know where the first syllable ends. The first three words are done for you. Here are three clues that will help you:

1. can / dy, mit / ten—vowel followed by two consonants and a vowel.

2. o / pen, bea / con, la / dy—vowel followed by a single consonant and a vowel.

3. bu / gle, rum / ble, strug / gle—final **le** preceded by a consonant.

1. el / bow ____1____   9. bundle _____

2. pi / lot ____2____   10. baby _____

3. shuf / fle ____3____   11. reason _____

4. wrinkle _____   12. corner _____

5. bugle _____   13. table _____

6. lazy _____   14. acorn _____

7. tiger _____   15. after _____

8. person _____

Name _____

Syllabication Review Activity 3

Practice 12

Directions: Look at each word below and decide where the first syllable ends. Draw a line between the first and second syllable of the word. Write the number of the clue listed below on the line next to each word to show how you know where the first syllable ends. Here are three clues that will help you:

1. can / dy, mit / ten—vowel followed by two consonants and a vowel.

2. o / pen, bea / con, la / dy—vowel followed by a single consonant and a vowel.

3. bu / gle, rum / ble, strug / gle—final **le** preceded by a consonant.

1. borrow _____   9. amble _____

2. cargo _____   10. tangle _____

3. nature _____   11. notice _____

4. tailor _____   12. iron _____

5. rifle _____   13. purple _____

6. captain _____   14. party _____

7. purpose _____   15. follow _____

8. simple _____

Name _____

Practice 13

Directions: Syllabicate the following words. Some examples are:

pi / lot   bub / ble
pea / nut   for / get
re / treat   poi / son
ca / ble   band / age

1. program _____

2. stardom _____

3. shameful _____

4. combat _____

5. raisin _____

6. lazy _____

7. corner _____

8. traffic _____

9. wrinkle _____

10. giggle _____

11. after _____

12. pepper _____

13. bundle _____

14. hobby _____

15. shuffle _____

Name _____

Practice 14

Directions: Syllabicate the following nonsense words.

1. prodeat _____   6. tripteme _____

2. dable _____   7. choaman _____

3. slapeme _____   8. faimat _____

4. brammle _____   9. cramo _____

5. shoitem _____   10. trotem _____

Name _____

Practice 15

Directions: Syllabicate the following words.

1. dentist _____   6. table _____

2. program _____   7. parade _____

3. manner _____   8. believe _____

4. baby _____   9. bundle _____

5. retreat _____   10. cradle _____

Name _____

Practice 16

Directions: Syllabicate the following nonsense words.

Examples:
di / lat
se / treat
poi / ret
pa / rate

1. proiteam _____

2. starpon _____

3. shamete _____

4. slaymene _____

5. dorlet _____

6. naimem _____

7. poiler _____

8. boimer _____

9. sladoil _____

10. datem _____

Name _____

Practice 17

Directions: First syllabicate the nonsense words. Then put in the accent marks.

Accent mark = (´) Place at end of stressed syllable.

Examples:
di´ / lat
pea´ / ton
se / treat´
poi´ / ret
pa / rate´

1. clameat _____

2. proidem _____

3. tomar _____

4. contoat _____

5. dromter _____

6. sureat _____

7. broiman _____

8. flagmene _____

9. modo _____

10. zampoit _____

Name _____

Practice 18

Directions: First syllabicate the words. Then put in the accent marks.

Accent mark = (´) Place at end of stressed syllable.

Examples:
pi´ / lot
pea´ / nut
bub´ / ble
cra´ / dle
re / treat´
poi´ / son

1. protest _____

2. lady _____

3. mittens _____

4. candle _____

5. iron _____

6. manners _____

7. replace _____

8. monkey _____

9. candy _____

10. penny _____

Name _____

Special Review Activity

Practice 19

Directions: First syllabicate the words. Then put in the accent marks.

Accent mark = (´) Place at end of stressed syllable.

Examples:
pi´ / lot
pea´ / nut
bub´ / ble
cra´ / dle
re / treat´
poi´ / son
re / cede´

1. cotton _____

2. traffic _____

3. lazy _____

4. rumble _____

5. silly _____

6. saddle _____

7. bottom _____

8. blister _____

9. maiden _____

10. repeat _____

Skill 2: Syllabication

Skinny Book: The Lion and the Mouse

On the following pages are reproducibles to make into a "Skinny Book." These Skinny Books are short, illustrated stories related to the presented skills. These small books are reproducible for distribution to children in classrooms or at home. The books are not only important time-savers for busy teachers but also important aids for parents who want to help their children succeed in learning to read.

Skinny Books are included in individual student books, which are available separately.

The Skinny Books are designed to be assembled easily to make individual Skinny Books for the children. If you do not have individual student books, you must first photocopy the pages you need for each child. Cut each page in half along the dotted line. Each page is numbered for ease of assembly. Place the pages in numerical order and staple the pages together along the left-hand side. Now you have a Skinny Book!

Make a copy for each child in your group. Children can color each page. You may also choose to make larger photocopies to make a Big Skinny Book for your "master copy." Or, ask student or adult volunteers to color and assemble each of the Skinny Book copies for you and keep a complete set for classroom use.

The Story

This is a fable about the Lion and the Mouse. Have the children follow along with you as you look at and read the Skinny Book together. Discuss each of the pages.

Page 1

The mouse runs across the sleeping lion. He wakes and roars.

Page 2

The mouse is scared and asks the lion not to eat him.

Page 3

The mouse says he will help the lion someday if he will not eat him.

Page 4

The lion thinks it's so funny that the mouse thinks he can help him.

Page 5

The lion laughs and lets the mouse go.

Page 6

The great lion gets caught in a hunter's net.

Page 7

The mouse hears the lion roaring and runs to help.

Page 8

The mouse tells the lion he will free him.

Page 9

The mouse chews the rope and frees the lion. The lion is grateful.

Pages 10 and 11

Words in the Skinny Book

Page 12

Study Question

Skill 3:

Word Families (Phonograms)

Explanation

Word families (phonograms) are a succession of letters that occurs with the same phonetic value in a number of words. All word families begin with a vowel, and all words that contain the same word family are spelled alike—they rhyme. As an example, the *ell* word family includes the words *bell, cell, fell, jell, Nell, sell, tell, well, yell, dwell, shell, smell, spell, swell,* and so on. The word families (phonograms) that we will be working with in this section are *ap, ate, ing, ill, ock, ent, ell, est, in,* and *y.*

Word families are especially helpful in both unlocking and building words. Working with larger word elements, such as word families, is often more helpful in decoding words than sounding out each consonant and vowel.

Special Notes

Some reading authorities fear that the use of word families will produce stories that are poor literature. In this text, however, the purpose is to help children learn how to effectively decode printed text as quickly as possible. Children enjoy seeing words they can read. And the use of word families is an excellent way to help children unlock and build hundreds of words.

Children also need reinforcement. They need to see words more than once in printed text in order to learn the words.

In teaching children about phonograms, teachers usually use the term *word families* with children rather than *phonograms.*

Teaching Strategies in Action

Teachers should help children recognize that they can build many words using word families. If children, for example, have learned the word *bell,* they can use this word to help them unlock many other words that also end in *ell.* The teacher presents children with the word *bell.* She then asks the children to change the letter *b* to another letter that sounds like the beginning of the word *win.* The teacher can then give the children a riddle to help them with the new word, for example—"This is where people can get water." (well)

Sample Practice

Here is a sample practice you can use with your students.

Directions: "The word *sing* is on the board. Let's see how many words we can make if we change the beginning letter. I'll give you two clues."

sing

The teacher then says, "If you change my first letter, you will be able to wear me on your finger. My first letter sounds like the beginning of *roll*."

Answer: ring

The teacher can continue giving children different riddles to make more words that fit the *ing* word family.

Modeling Strategy

Here is how one teacher models for her children how to unlock an unfamiliar word that has the same word family that they have already met in a different word. When the teacher reads aloud the following sentences on the board, she stumbles on the word *shell*:

The man found a *shell* on the beach.

The teacher says to the children that she will say aloud how she figures out the word she stumbled on. She says, "I don't know this word. However, I do know the word *bell*. It looks like the word I don't know and the word *bell* come from the same word family—the *ell* word family. I know that word families rhyme. I also know that the word I don't know begins with *sh*, as in the word *ship*. If I put the consonant digraph *sh* in place of the letter *b* in the word *bell*, I'll have the word *shell*. Let me see if it makes sense in the sentence."

After the teacher reads aloud the sentence pronouncing the word *shell* correctly, she says, "Yes, it does make sense. The man found a shell on the beach. The beach is a place where we can find shells."

Learning Objectives

❑ To be able to build and decode words in the *ap* word family (practices 1–5).

❑ To be able to build and decode words in the *ate* word family (practices 6–10).

❑ To be able to build and decode words in the *ing* word family (practices 11–15).

❑ To be able to build and decode words in the *ill* word family (practices 16–18).

❑ To be able to build and decode words in the *ock* word family (practices 19–21).

❑ To be able to build and decode words in the *ent* word family (practices 22–23).

❑ To be able to build and decode words in the *ell* word family (practices 24–25).

❑ To be able to build and decode words in the *est* word family (practices 26–27).

❑ To be able to build and decode words in the *in* word family (practices 28–29).

❑ To be able to build and decode words in the *y* word family (practices 30–31).

Directions for Student Practices

Use the student practices (pages 113–143) to help your children acquire, reinforce, and review word families. Pick and choose the practices based on the needs and developmental levels of your students. Answers for the student practice pages are on pages 164–166.

IMPORTANT:

When working with word families, you should do the practices with the children. Have the children listen carefully as you read the directions to them. You may need to repeat the directions for your students as you do the practices. This depends on the individual differences of the students.

Extensions

Rhyme Time

Invite children to begin clapping their hands. Choose a child to say a word family, such as *ent*. That child points to another child who then, while still clapping, must give another word that rhymes with *ent*. For example, the first child says the word *bent* and points to another child. The second child says the word *gent* and points to another child. The third child says *sent* and points to another child, and so forth. When a child cannot think of a word from that word family that is a member of the particular word family in play, you can initiate another word family.

Word Family Bulletin Board

Create a word family bulletin board. Place the word families you are working with at the top of the bulletin board. For example, place "___ ing," "___ ate," and "___ ill" at the top. Invite children to cut pictures from magazines as well as draw pictures that illustrate the words in the word families, such as pictures of *ring, king, crate, skate, pill, hill*, and so on. Display the children's illustrations and pictures below the appropriate word families.

Memory Game

Have available a deck of cards with words from the *ap, ate, ing, ill, ock, ent, ell, est, in,* and *y* word families. Place each card face down on a table. A child picks two cards. He or she must state whether the cards are from the same word family. If they are, the child keeps the set. If not, the child turns both cards face down again. Play continues until there are no more cards left on the table. The child with the greatest number of matches is the winner.

Spelling Fun

Invite children to learn new words. For example, while children are learning the word family *est*, and have already worked with most initial consonants and consonant substitution, they can also learn to spell a number of other words in the *est* family, such as *best, test, chest*, and so on. These words can be put into sentences and illustrated by the children.

Word Endings

This is a more difficult game. Help children learn a very useful spelling generalization that deals with words that end in one consonant and have one vowel only. For example, when the children are learning word families, such as *ap* and *in*, they can also learn that before they add an ending beginning with a vowel, such as *ed or ing*, they usually should double the final consonant. For example, *wrap* becomes *wrapping*, *pin* becomes *pinned*, and so on. Ask one child to come up with a word with one vowel that ends with one consonant. Then ask another child to add *ed* or *ing* to the word. Practice the game and then have children add endings to words, such as *rap, cap, pin, grin*, and so on.

Create a Story

Create word-family silly stories with the children. On a pad of chart paper, place one sentence of the story on each sheet, leaving space at the bottom. Begin by suggesting a word family to the children, for example, *ing*. Then start the story with a sentence containing a word in that family, such as

"The *string* was taking a walk." Add sentences to the story using words in the same word family. "The *string* turned into a *fling* and ran away," and so on. Continue the story, writing each sentence on a page. Help children make up an ending for their story as well. Then start at the beginning and have individual children volunteer to read aloud each page of the story. Invite children to illustrate each of the sentences. You may want to display your group story on the bulletin board and share it with the children's families.

Student's Name _____

Assessment Tool Progress Report

Progress

Improvement

Comments

Name _____

Practice 1

Directions: Here are words from the **ap** word family. Add one or more letters to the beginning of **ap** to make a word that fits the clues I say aloud.

Let's do one together. Here are two clues. "You use me to help you find where you are going. I begin like the word **man**." I put the letter **m** in front of **ap**, and it becomes the word **map**. I see that the word **map** fits my clues. Let's make more words that rhyme with **map** that belong to the **ap** word family.

ap
map

1. _____ ap   I am something that comes from trees. I begin like the word **sun**.

2. _____ ap   I can hold things on me when I am sitting down. I begin like the word **lake**.

3. _____ ap   I can do this with my fingers. I begin like the word **snow**.

4. _____ ap   You wear me on your head. I begin like the word **cook**.

5. _____ ap   You do this to gifts. I begin like the word **write**.

6. _____ ap   I am another word for "hit." I begin like the word **slip**.

7. _____ ap   Babies take this when they are tired. I begin like the word **not**.

8. _____ ap   This refers to a man. I begin like the word **chair**.

9. _____ ap   Hunters can do this to a lion. I begin like the word **trip**.

10. _____ ap   After we watch a show, we do this. I begin like the word **club**.

Name _____

Practice 2

Directions: Here are words from the **ap** word family. Write the correct word in the space next to its picture.

cap   clap   lap   map   strap   trap

1.  _____

2.  _____

3.  _____

4.  _____

5.  _____

6.  _____

Name _____

Practice 3

Directions: Here are words from the **ap** word family. Each sentence below is missing a word. Write the correct word in the space. A word may be used only once.

cap   clap   lap   map   nap   scrap   snap   strap   trap   wrap

1. Lisa is holding lots of things on her _____.

2. At school, we have a _____ that shows all the states in the United States.

3. My baby brother takes a _____ in his crib.

4. My dog will not eat a _____ of our leftover food.

5. We need to _____ Kelsey's presents.

6. My dress has one _____ at the back of it.

7. Everyone will _____ at the end of the play if they like it.

8. Put your _____ back on your head.

9. The man uses a _____ to hold up his pants.

10. Will you use a _____ to catch the mouse in your house?

Name _____

Practice 4

Directions: Here is a silly story. It has lots of words from the **ap** word family. Read the story. Write an ending for the story.

Kelsey's Magic Cap

Kelsey had a cap.

It was a magic cap.

The cap could become a strap, a map, a lap or a chap.

The magic cap could even take a nap.

The cap could flap in the wind.

It could clap and even rap and tap.

The cap didn't like to be wrapped.

When Kelsey tried to wrap her cap, the cap

ran away.

"No one can wrap me," said the cap.

"I can't be in a trap.

I'm a magic cap.

I can be anything I want to be.

No one can put me in a box.

I won't go. No, no, no!"

Finish the story of "Kelsey's Magic Cap."

_____

_____

_____

_____

Name _____

Practice 5

Directions: Here are some sentences. Some of the sentences are silly. Some of them are not silly. Write "silly" if the sentence is silly. Write "not silly" if the sentence is not silly.

1. A cap can talk. _____

2. You wear a cap on your head. _____

3. A cap can be green or yellow. _____

4. A girl can wear a cap. _____

5. Some caps can wrap themselves. _____

6. A cap can run away. _____

7. A cap can tap and clap. _____

8. A cap can read a map. _____

9. A cap can be big or small. _____

10. A child can have lots of caps. _____

Name _____

Practice 6

Directions: Here are words from the **ate** word family. Add one or more letters to the beginning of **ate** to make a word that fits the clues I say aloud.

Let's do one together. Here are two clues. "I am used in a fireplace. I begin like the word **grab**." I put the letters **gr** in front of **ate**, and it becomes the word **grate**. I see that the word **grate** fits my clues. Let's make more words that rhyme with **grate** that belong to the **ate** word family.

ate
grate

1. _____ ate   I am never on time. I begin like the word **let**.

2. _____ ate   I am a girl's name. I begin like the word **king**.

3. _____ ate   I am something on a calendar. I begin like the word **dog**.

4. _____ ate   I can keep people from getting in or out. I begin like the word **go**.

5. _____ ate   I do not like people. I begin like the word **hot**.

6. _____ ate   You eat off me. I begin like the word **plant**.

7. _____ ate   This is fun to do. I begin like the word **sky**.

8. _____ ate   There are fifty of these in the United States. I begin like the word **step**.

9. _____ ate   I am one of a pair. I begin like the word **mat**.

10. _____ ate   I am a container used for storing things. I begin like the word **crawl**.

Name _____

Practice 7

Directions: Here are words from the **ate** word family. Write the correct word in the space next to its picture.

crate   date   gate   Kate   plate   skate   state

1. _____

2. _____

3. _____

4. _____

5. _____

6. _____

7. _____

119

Name _____

Practice 8

Directions: Here are words from the **ate** word family. Each sentence below is missing a word. Write the correct word in the space. A word may be used only once.

**ate   crate   date   fate   gate   hate   Kate   plate
skate   state**

1. Lee said that he _____ all the chips.

2. It's _____ that we meet again.

3. Please close the _____ so my dog will not run away.

4. What do you have in that _____?

5. _____ is a nice name for a girl.

6. Did you eat all the vegetables on your _____?

7. The _____ for the party is April 24th.

8. Do you wear a helmet when you _____?

9. What _____ do you live in?

10. It is better to love people than to _____ them.

Name _____

Practice 9

Directions: Here is a silly story. It has lots of words from the **ate** word family. Read the story. Write an ending for the story and draw a picture.

 A Silly Story

This story is about Kate and her mate who loved to eat dates.

Together they ate and ate lots of dates.

They ate little dates. They ate big dates.

One day they ate one hundred dates.

Kate and her mate always cleaned their plates.

When it came to good things to eat, Kate and her mate would

    hate to be late.

They liked to skate. Once they won the skate contest in their state.

Their prize came in a big crate.

Can you guess what came in the crate? Write an ending to this silly story.

Draw a picture about your story ending on another sheet of paper.

121

Name _____

Practice 10

Directions: Here are some sentences. Some of the sentences are silly. Some of them are not silly. Write "silly" if the sentence is silly. Write "not silly" if the sentence is not silly.

1. A skate can eat dates. _____

2. A date is something you can eat. _____

3. There are fifty states in the United States. _____

4. A plate is something you eat on. _____

5. A gate can swing. _____

6. You are early if you are late. _____

7. A plate can talk. _____

8. A state can walk and talk. _____

9. Kate can play games. _____

10. Crates hold things in them. _____

Name _____

Practice 11

Directions: Here are words from the **ing** word family. Add one or more letters to the beginning of **ing** to make a word that fits the clues I say aloud.

Let's do one together. Here are two clues: "I do this with my voice. I begin like the word **see**." I put the letter **s** in front of **ing**, and it becomes the word **sing**. I see that the word **sing** fits my clues. Let's make more words that rhyme with **sing** that belong to the **ing** word family.

ing
sing

1. _____ ing   A bird has me. I begin like the word **went**.

2. _____ ing   You wear me on your finger. I begin like the word **rose**.

3. _____ ing   I live in a castle. I begin like the word **kite**.

4. _____ ing   You do this to a gift when you go to a party. I begin like the word **bread**.

5. _____ ing   I wore this when I broke my arm. I begin like the word **slap**.

6. _____ ing   I am a season. I begin like the word **spread**.

7. _____ ing   I am used to tie things. I begin like the word **straw**.

8. _____ ing   A bee can do this. I begin like the word **step**.

9. _____ ing   I can go high on this. I begin like the word **swish**.

10. _____ ing   I am an object. I begin like the word **thin**.

123

Name _____

Practice 12

Directions: Here are words from the **ing** word family. Write the correct word in the space next to its picture. There are more words listed than you will need.

**bring   earring   fling   king   ring   sling   sting
string   swing   thing   wing**

1. _____

2. _____

3. _____

4. _____

5. _____

6. _____

7. _____

Name _____

Practice 13

Directions: Here are words from the **ing** word family. Each sentence below is missing a word. Write the correct word in the space. A word may be used only once.

> **fling   king   ring   sling   spring   sting   string**
> **swing   wing   wring**

1. I always wear this _____ on my finger.

2. My favorite season is _____.

3. Please _____ the towel to get rid of the water.

4. The _____ lives in a castle.

5. Did the bird hurt its _____?

6. The bee did not _____ me.

7. Please push me high on the _____.

8. I will tie the box with _____.

9. Bob broke his arm and had it in a _____.

10. Do not _____ your pen across the room.

Name _____

Practice 14

Directions: Here is a silly story. It has lots of words from the **ing** word family. Read the story. Write an ending for the story. Then write two questions for the story.

A Silly Story

One spring day, Jill found a ring.
The ring belonged to the king.
Jill set out to bring the ring to the king.
On the way, she met a bird.
The bird was on a swing.
"Push me high. Push me high," said the bird to Jill.
"I can't," Jill said.
"I'm on my way to see the king. I found his ring."
"Oh, let me go with you," said the bird.
"I can sing and hold the ring on my wing."
"Oh, no," Jill said. "I do not want to lose this
    ring. I have tied a string to the ring. See, I am pulling it
    along on the ground."
Jill and the bird, and the ring walked on.
Just then, they heard a voice say, "Where are you going?"
"We are going to the castle to see the king.
We have his ring," said Jill and the bird.
"Oh, oh, let me go with you!" cried the frog.
"All right," said Jill, "but you must walk fast.
We are on our way to the king and it is getting
    dark. It is getting late."

Finish the story on a separate sheet of paper. Then make up two questions about the story.

Questions:

1. _____

2. _____

Name _____

Practice 15

Directions: Here are some sentences. Some of the sentences are silly. Some of them are not silly. Write "silly" if the sentence is silly. Write "not silly" if the sentence is not silly.

1. Birds and frogs can talk. _____

2. Girls and boys can talk. _____

3. A bee can sting you. _____

4. Spring is a season. _____

5. Frogs have wings. _____

6. Frogs can fly in the sky. _____

7. When you wring something dry, you make it wet. _____

8. Spring can mean "to jump." _____

9. Bring means "to go away." _____

10. Rings are round. _____

Name _____

Practice 16

Directions: Here are words from the **ill** word family. Add one or more letters to the beginning of **ill** to make a word that fits the clues I say aloud.

Let's do one together. Here are some clues. "I am a name and you also need to pay me. I begin like the word **baby**." I put the letter **b** in front of **ill**, and it becomes the word **Bill** or **bill**. I see that the words **Bill** and **bill** fit my clues. Let's make more words that rhyme with **bill** that belong to the **ill**, word family.

ill
bill

1. _____ ill   I'm the name of a girl in a nursery rhyme. I begin like the word **jam**.

2. _____ ill   I'm something you take when you are sick. I begin like the word **put**.

3. _____ ill   I mean "sick." Do not add any letters to me.

4. _____ ill   Fish have me. I begin like the word **got**.

5. _____ ill   I'm a place for grinding grain into flour. I begin like the word **milk**.

6. _____ ill   I get this when I am in a draft. I begin like the word **champ**.

7. _____ ill   I'm steep. I begin like the word **hot**.

8. _____ ill   I have ability in something. I begin like the word **skip**.

9. _____ ill   I'm a tool for making holes. I begin like the word **drip**.

10. _____ ill   I give great delight to people. I begin like the word **throw**.

Name _____

Practice 17

Directions: Here are some sentences. Some of the sentences are silly. Some of them are not silly. Write "silly" if the sentence is silly. Write "not silly" if the sentence is not silly.

1. A frill is something that flies in the sky. _____

2. A mill is a place to go swimming. _____

3. A hill can cook. _____

4. You are hot when you have a chill. _____

5. A dog has a gill. _____

6. The doctor can give a sick person a pill. _____

7. When you are still, you are moving and making a lot of noise.

   _____

8. A skill is something you eat. _____

9. You can cook on a grill. _____

10. Jack and Jill can go up a hill. _____

11. A drill can cook on a grill and walk up a hill. _____

12. A child can spill milk on a window sill. _____

Name _____

Practice 18

Directions: Choose a word from the word list to fit the sentence. A word may be used only once. There are more words than you need.

bill   chill   drill   fill   hill   ill   pill   quill   spill
still   thrill   will

1. I _____ not go to her house later.

2. It was a _____ to meet such a famous person.

3. The draft is giving me a _____.

4. When I am sick, my doctor gives me a _____.

5. Did your mother call the doctor when you were _____?

6. Try not to _____ anything on your clothes.

7. Did you pay your _____ yet?

8. Please _____ some holes in the wood.

9. Be _____ when you are at the movies.

10. We have to walk up a big _____ to get to Jill's house.

Name _____

Practice 19

Directions: Here are words from the **ock** word family. Add one or more letters to the beginning of **ock** to make a word that fits the clues I say aloud.

Let's do one together. Here are two clues. "Children can build with me. I begin like the word **blue**." I put the letters **bl** in front of **ock**, and it becomes the word **block**. I see that the word **block** fits my clues. Let's make more words that rhyme with **block** that belong to the **ock** word family.

ock
block

1. _____ ock   You do this to doors. I begin like the word **let**.

2. _____ ock   You wear me. I begin like the word **sad.**

3. _____ ock   I give you the time. I begin like the word **clip**.

4. _____ ock   I do this on a door before I come in. I begin like the word **know**.

5. _____ ock   I am where ships load or unload. I begin like the word **deck**.

6. _____ ock   I am a group of animals that live together. I begin like the word **floor**.

7. _____ ock   I am a dress. I begin like the word **fry**.

8. _____ ock   Storekeepers keep me so they will not run out of things to sell. I begin like the word **stop**.

9. _____ ock   I'm very hard. I begin like the word **red**.

10. _____ ock   You wear me when you paint. I begin like the word **smoke**.

Name _____

Practice 20

Directions: Here are some sentences. Some of the sentences are silly. Some of them are not silly. Write "silly" if the sentence is silly. Write "not silly" if the sentence is not silly.

1. Clocks can fly. _____

2. A hard rock is soft. _____

3. You wear a sock on your foot. _____

4. You put a lock on a nose. _____

5. Birds wear frocks. _____

6. Children build with blocks. _____

7. You should knock before entering someone's room. _____

8. It's not nice to mock people. _____

9. A flock of birds fly alone. _____

10. When you stock up on something, you have lots of it. _____

Name _____

Practice 21

Directions: Choose a word from the word list to fit the sentence. A word may be used only once.

**block   clock   dock   frock   knock   lock   rock
smock   sock   stock**

1. Does the store have a large _____ of clothes?

2. What a pretty _____ the woman is wearing.

3. The ships unloaded at the _____.

4. Look at the _____ and tell me what time it is.

5. Always _____ before you enter my room.

6. When I paint, I always wear a _____ over my clothes to keep them clean.

7. My house is on that _____.

8. You still need to put one shoe and _____ on.

9. I fell on a large, sharp _____ and hurt my knee.

10. Please _____ the house when you leave.

Name _____

Practice 22

Directions: Here are words from the **ent** word family. Add one or more letters to the beginning of **ent** to make a word that fits the clues I say aloud.

Let's do one together. Here are two clues. "You can sleep in me on a camping trip. I begin like the word **top**." I put the letter **t** in front of **ent**, and it becomes the word **tent**. I see that the word **tent** fits my clues. Let's make more words that rhyme with **tent** that belong to the **ent** word family.

ent
tent

1. _____ ent   I am a crooked shape when I am this. I begin like the word **book**.

2. _____ ent   I am a boy's name. I begin like the word **king**.

3. _____ ent   I am a penny. I begin like the word **center**.

4. _____ ent   I am a polite man. I begin like the word **gentle**.

5. _____ ent   I was told to go someplace yesterday. I begin like the word **so**.

6. _____ ent   I left yesterday. I begin like the word **wet**.

7. _____ ent   I am a smell. I begin like the word **scene**.

8. _____ ent   I did this with my money. I begin like the word **spin**.

9. _____ ent   I pay money for an apartment. I begin like the word **red**.

10. _____ ent   I let someone borrow something from me yesterday. I begin like the word **let**.

Name _____

Practice 23

Directions: Choose a word from the word list to fit the sentence. A word may be used only once.

**bent   cent   dent   lent   rent   sent   scent   spent
tent   went**

1. The old man with the _____ back walked slowly.

2. Kent needs one more _____ to pay for the candy.

3. We will sleep in a large _____ when we go on our trip to the woods.

4. The rock hit my mother's car and made a big _____ in it.

5. How much _____ is it to live in this building?

6. The _____ of the flowers is very nice.

7. I _____ a letter to my grandmother and grandfather yesterday.

8. We _____ to our grandparents' house yesterday.

9. My father _____ his friend his tools last week.

10. We _____ all our money and have nothing left.

Name _____

Practice 24

Directions: Here are words from the **ell** word family. Add one or more letters to the beginning of **ell** to make a word that fits the clues I say aloud.

Let's do one together. Here are two clues. "I am this when I feel fine. I begin like the word **wall**." I put the letter **w** in front of **ell**, and it becomes the word **well**. I see that the word **well** fits my clues. Let's make more words that rhyme with **well** that belong to the **ell** word family.

ell
well

1. _____ ell   You can get water from me. I begin like the word **watch**.

2. _____ ell   I do this in my shop. I begin like the word **sick**.

3. _____ ell   I ring. I begin like the word **book**.

4. _____ ell   I got hurt when I did this. I begin like the word **fat**.

5. _____ ell   When Jell-O gelatin is in the refrigerator, it does this. I begin like the word **jam**.

6. _____ ell   I mean "to live someplace." I begin like the word **dwarf**.

7. _____ ell   I feel this way when something good happens. I begin like the word **swim**.

8. _____ ell   To write words correctly, I need to know how to do this. I begin like the word **Spain**.

9. _____ ell   I am another word for "scent." I begin like the word **smart**.

Name _____

Practice 25

Directions: Choose a word from the word list to fit the sentence. A word may be used only once.

bell   fell   jell   sell   shell   smell   spell   tell
well   yell

1. It hurts my ears when you _____ so loudly.

2. We found a big _____ on the beach.

3. Will the Jell-O _____ in time for lunch?

4. Please _____ us what happened.

5. Are you feeling _____?

6. Do you know how to _____ this word?

7. Someone is ringing the _____.

8. What is that awful _____?

9. The child _____ and broke his arm.

10. The storekeeper said that he would _____ all his stock by next week.

Name _____

Practice 26

Directions: Here are words from the **est** word family. Add one or more letters to the beginning of **est** to make a word that fits the clues I say aloud.

Let's do one together. Here are two clues. "I need this when I am tired. I begin like the word **rag**." I put the letter **r** in front of **est**, and it becomes the word **rest**. I see that the word **rest** fits my clues. Let's make more words that rhyme with **rest** that belong to the **est** word family.

est
rest

1. _____ est   I am a direction. I begin like the word **well**.

2. _____ est   I am this person when I visit someone. I begin like the word **guess**.

3. _____ est   No one is better than I am. I begin like the word **bet**.

4. _____ est   Birds live in me. I begin like the word **not**.

5. _____ est   I take this at school to see how well I do. I begin like the word **to**.

6. _____ est   I bother people. I begin like the word **pet**.

7. _____ est   You can wear me. I begin like the word **van**.

8. _____ est   I am part of your body. I begin like the word **chair**.

Name _____

Practice 27

Directions: Choose a word from the word list to fit the sentence. A word may be used only once.

**best   chest   guest   nest   pest   rest   test
vest   west**

1. Do you always wear a _____ with your jacket?

2. Should I go east or _____ to get to your house?

3. That is the _____ pie I have ever eaten.

4. Who will be your _____ next weekend?

5. I love my little brother, but sometimes he bothers me and is a

_____.

6. Do we have a math _____ tomorrow?

7. I have a cold in my _____.

8. What a beautiful _____ the robin built.

9. After the long walk, we all needed a _____.

Name _____

Practice 28

Directions: Here are words from the **in** word family. Add one or more letters to the beginning of **in** to make a word that fits the clues I say aloud.

Let's do one together. Here are two clues. "I use this to hold something together. I begin like the word **pail**." I put the letter **p** in front of **in**, and it becomes the word **pin**. I see that the word **pin** fits my clues. Let's make more words that rhyme with **pin** that belong to the **in** word family.

in
pin

1. _____ in   I am the opposite of **lose**. I begin like the word **wall**.

2. _____ in   I am the opposite of **fat**. I begin like the word **thick**.

3. _____ in   I am a relative. I begin like the word **king**.

4. _____ in   A fish has me. I begin like the word **find**.

5. _____ in   I am a metal. I begin like the word **top**.

6. _____ in   There are two of us. I begin like the word **twelve**.

7. _____ in   I am part of your face. I begin like the word **chair**.

8. _____ in   I cover all of you. I begin like the word **skip**.

9. _____ in   I do this when I am happy. I begin like the word **grab**.

10. _____ in   I am part of your leg. I begin like the word **ship**.

Name _____

Practice 29

Directions: Choose a word from the word list to fit the sentence. A word may be used only once.

> **fin   grin   in   pin   shin   skin   spin   thin**
> **twin   win**

1. Did a spider _____ that web?

2. I hurt the _____ of my leg.

3. Is it fun to have a _____ who looks just like you?

4. That sweater is so _____, you must be cold.

5. I would like to go _____ now.

6. When I touched the hot stove, I burned the _____ on my arm.

7. I like to _____ when I play games.

8. I need a _____ to hold my hem in place.

9. Why do you always have a silly _____ on your face?

10. The fish can't swim with only one _____.

Name _____

Practice 30

Directions: Here are words from the **y** (long **i**) word family. When the **y** is at the end of a one-syllable word, and there are no other vowels in the word, the **y** sounds like long **i**. Add one or more letters to the beginning of **y** to make a word that fits the clues I say aloud.

Let's do one together. Here are two clues. "A bird can do this. I begin like the word **flag**." I put the letters **fl** in front of **y**, and it becomes the word **fly**. I see that the word **fly** fits my clues. Let's make more words that rhyme with **fly** and belong to the **y** word family.

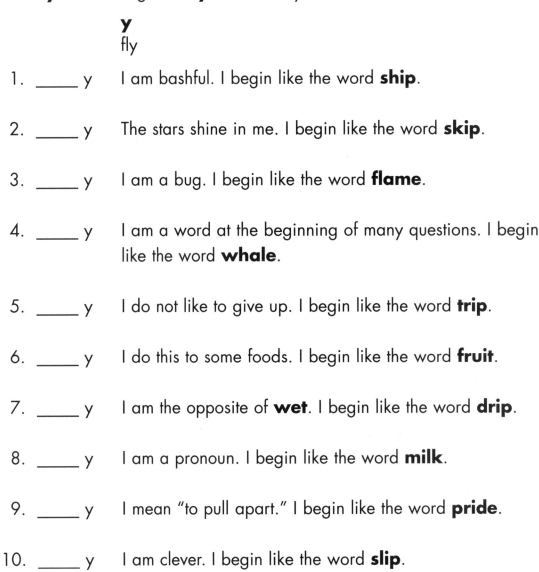

y
fly

1. _____ y   I am bashful. I begin like the word **ship**.

2. _____ y   The stars shine in me. I begin like the word **skip**.

3. _____ y   I am a bug. I begin like the word **flame**.

4. _____ y   I am a word at the beginning of many questions. I begin like the word **whale**.

5. _____ y   I do not like to give up. I begin like the word **trip**.

6. _____ y   I do this to some foods. I begin like the word **fruit**.

7. _____ y   I am the opposite of **wet**. I begin like the word **drip**.

8. _____ y   I am a pronoun. I begin like the word **milk**.

9. _____ y   I mean "to pull apart." I begin like the word **pride**.

10. _____ y   I am clever. I begin like the word **slip**.

Name _____

Practice 31

Directions: Choose a word from the word list to fit the sentence. A word may be used only once.

cry   dry   fly   fry   my   pry   shy   sky   sly   spy

1. Have you seen _____ slippers?

2. Today the _____ is blue, without a cloud in it.

3. Your eyes become filled with tears when you _____.

4. Will you _____ that in oil?

5. It must be nice to _____ like a bird.

6. Here is a towel to _____ your hands.

7. Be careful of Jill because she is very tricky and _____.

8. Lee is outgoing, but his sister is very _____.

9. It's not nice to _____ into other people's business.

10. Who told you to secretly _____ on him?

Word Families

Skinny Book: The Town Mouse and the Country Mouse

On the following pages are reproducibles to make into a "Skinny Book." These Skinny Books are short, illustrated stories related to the presented skills. These small books are reproducible for distribution to children in classrooms or at home. The books are not only important time-savers for busy teachers but also important aids for parents who want to help their children succeed in learning to read.

Skinny Books are included in individual workbooks, which are available separately.

The Skinny Books are designed to be assembled easily to make individual Skinny Books for the children. If you do not have individual workbooks, you must first photocopy the pages you need for each child. Cut each page in half along the dotted line. Each page is numbered for ease of assembly. Place the pages in numerical order and staple the pages together along the left-hand side. Now you have a Skinny Book!

Make a copy for each child in your group. Children can color each page. You may also choose to make larger photocopies to make a Big Skinny Book for your "master copy." Or, ask student or adult volunteers to color and assemble each of the Skinny Book copies for you and keep a complete set for classroom use.

The Story

This is a fable about the Town Mouse and the Country Mouse. Have the children follow along with you as you look at and read the Skinny Book together. Discuss each of the pages.

Page 1
The Country Mouse is in his plain house.

Page 2
The Town Mouse is all dressed up, visiting the Country Mouse.

Page 3
The Country Mouse greets the Town Mouse.

Page 4
The Country Mouse gives the Town Mouse lots of good, plain food to eat.

Page 5

The Country Mouse and The Town Mouse journey to the city.

Page 6

They arrive at the Town Mouse's house, which is very large and grand.

Page 7

The Country Mouse and the Town Mouse walk on their tiptoes.

Page 8

A dining room table is filled with lots of fancy things to eat.

Page 9

The Town Mouse and the Country Mouse are eating when a cat, dog, and people enter.

Page 10

The Country Mouse and the Town Mouse run away from the dog and cat.

Page 11

The Country Mouse says good-bye to the Town Mouse.

Page 12

Study Question

Words in Skinny Book

See page 153.

Name _____

Words in Skinny Book:

The Country Mouse and the Town Mouse

a	came	fast	hungry	might	said	too
act	can	fear	hurry	more	saw	took
after	can't	feasted	I	mouse	say	town
agree	care	feather	I'd	mouse's	scared	train
all	cat	few	I'm	much	see	two
all's	catching	filled	in	must	seen	up
also	city	finally	inside	my	sense	us
always	clean	fine	into	need	shiny	used
am	close	flew	is	needed	shirt	very
and	clothes	followed	it	never	shock	visit
answered	come	food	it's	next	shush	wake
any	continued	for	I've	no	silk	walked
anyone	corner	fun	jacket	not	simple	walking
anything	could	gave	just	nothing	sleeves	want
are	country	get	large	notice	small	wanted
around	cousin	glad	late	now	so	was
as	day	go	left	of	soon	way
asked	didn't	good	let's	offered	some	we
at	dining	good-bye	life	oh	started	well
ate	do	got	like	on	starving	went
away	dog	grand	liked	one	such	were
bad	don't	green	live	open	sure	what
bark	door	had	lives	out	surprised	when
barking	dressed	hadn't	lived	pants	table	while
basket	dull	happy	long	peace	than	whiskers
because	eat	hat	look	people	that	whispered
before	eating	have	looking	place	the	who
be	else	he	lot	plain	their	wide
being	end	here	lots	please	them	with
big	ends	hiding	made	quiet	then	women
blocks	escape	him	may	ran	they	word
body	especially	his	me	rather	things	wore
bone	everything	hole	men	reached	think	worth
both	expect	home	mean	red	this	wouldn't
but	explain	house	meow	room	time	yes
call	eyes	how	meowing	ruffles	tiptoes	you
calls	fancy	however	mice	rude	to	

Phonics IV: Skills Checklist Diagnostic Assessment

On the following pages is a post test based on the material presented in this book. This post-assessment tool is for individual administration. If a child misses two items from a skill area on this assessment, the teacher should present the child with relevant practices from Levels 1, 2, 3, or 4 Phonics for review purposes.

Student's Name:

Grade :

Teacher:

General Directions: Based on the specific item being assessed, the teacher can put either a check in the relevant box if the child gets it correct or insert the child's incorrect answer(s) in the box.

Auditory Discrimination

1. The student is able to listen to a set of words and state which pairs are the same:

		YES	NO
Ted	Ted		
cap	cap		
bud	but		
out	out		
shell	shall		
bit	bet		
send	sand		

2. The student is able to listen to a word and state another word that begins like:

	YES	NO
boy		
ran		
mine		
pencil		

3. The student is able to listen to a word and state another word that ends like:

	YES	NO
clock		
hat		
card		
plum		

4. The student can state another word that rhymes with:

	YES	NO
ham		
fat		
tan		
bake		
game		
tag		

5. The student can give the letter that stands for the first
sound heard in:

    bury

    mother

    zone

    curb

    label

    jewel

    yell

YES	NO

6. The student can give the two letters that stand for
the first two sounds heard in:

    plan

    twin

    stone

    swan

    float

    snag

    cry

    glove

7. The student can give the two letters that stand
for the first sound heard in:

    chair

    shame

    thumb

    phone

8. The student can give the letter that stands for the last
sound heard in:

    plan

    mom

    rug

    car

    buzz

    tub

Visual Discrimination

1. Following are a number of letters. The student is able to choose the letter that is different from the first one in the line:

    Example: E E **D** E E

        a. U R U U U U
        b. P P P P P D
        c. d d d b d d
        d. p p p p d p

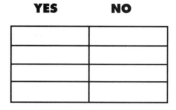

2. Following are a number of words. The student is able to choose the word that is the same as the first word:

    Example: big bag get **big** beg bug

    a. won   now   own   won   was   war

    b. saw   son   saw   son   sow   sun

    c. fun   far   fat   fan   fin   fun

    d. noon   none   nine   noon   neon   name

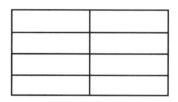

Word Analysis – Auditory

1. The student is able to state the number of syllables in each word:

    ("Listen carefully. Each of the words I am going to pronounce has one or more than one syllable. Tell me the number of syllables you hear in each word.")

        a. peanut   (2)
        b. candy   (2)
        c. cook   (1)
        d. run   (1)
        e. reached   (1)
        f. flower   (2)
        g. baby   (2)
        h. cake   (1)

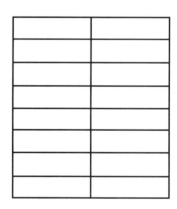

2. The student is able to state the vowel sound he or she hears in each word:

("Listen carefully. Tell me the vowel sound you hear in each word.")

	YES	NO
a. bake (ā)		
b. coat (ō)		
c. pit (ĭ)		
d. hen (ĕ)		
e. bat (ă)		
f. use (ū)		
g. leap (ē)		
h. neck (ĕ)		
i. pine (ī)		
j. lip (ĭ)		

Word Analysis - Visual

The student is able to pronounce the following nonsense words:
("Can you pronounce the following nonsense words?")

a. trat (trăt)		
b. po (pō)		
c. loap (lōap)		
d. hake (hāke)		
e. chine (chīne)		
f. phat (făt)		
g. lipo (līpō)		
h. roin (roin)		

Special Diagnostic Phonics Assessment

Use the following diagnostic assessment to evaluate your students' work in phonics. This assessment will help you understand where your students are in their learning, as well as what areas you may need to go over again with the children.

Student's Name:

Grade :

Teacher:

Part 1

1. Here are a number of nonsense words. Syllabicate each one.
   a. drutter
   b. cady
   c. thodman
   d. maddle
   e. trotmer
   f. minter

2. Here are a number of nonsense syllables. Circle the syllable in each set that does not belong. Explain why it does not belong.
   a. at   sem   ant   fo
   b. tle   mle   le   sle
   c. ai   ay   oy   ea
   d. klot   shom   tret   slib
   e. cen   kon   rom   sar

Part 2

1. Which of the following is not a syllable?
   a. t
   b. al
   c. a
   d. be

2. Which of the following is a syllable?
   a. m
   b. tul
   c. br
   d. ch

3. Which of the following are examples of consonant blends?
   a. bl   tr   c. ee   ai
   b. ch   sh   d. t   b

4. Consonant digraphs are:
   a. bl tr   c. oa ea
   b. b   t   d. th sh

5. Examples of silent consonants are:
   a. dr st   c. wr kn
   b. bl tr   d. sh ch

6. Long vowel sounds exist in:
   a. me   so   c. hid   hat
   b. set   lamp   d. none of the above.

7. Short vowel sounds exist in:
   a. shame   tire
   b. shut   set
   c. boat   sail
   d. may   car

8. Which word follows the "silent e" rule?
   a. toy   c. cat
   b. go   d. take

9. The letter *y* represents a long vowel sound in:
   a. yet   c. toy
   b. my   d. young

10. An example of a word with a diphthong (a double vowel in which both vowels are heard) is:
    a. boat   c. but
    b. my   d. boy

11. Which one of the following is a diphthong (a double vowel in which both vowels are heard)?
    a. ai   c. ea
    b. ee   d. oy

12. Which one of the following words contains a vowel digraph (a double vowel with one vowel sound)?
    a. mouse   c. house
    b. rain   d. boy

13. Which one of the following is a syllable?
    a. th   c. tr
    b. r   d. cro

14. Which word is a one-syllable word?
    a. saddle   c. girl
    b. candy   d. pilot

15. Which word is a two-syllable word?
    a. baby   c. dog
    b. boy   d. clown

16. Which is the correct syllabication of *bottem?*
    a. bot / tem
    b. bo / ttem
    c. bott / em
    d. botte / m

17. Which is the correct syllabication of *crono?*
    a. cr / ono
    b. cro / no
    c. c / rono
    d. cron / o

18. Which is the correct syllabication of *roble?*
    a. ro / ble
    b. rob / le
    c. robl / e
    d. r / oble

19. The words *sunlight* and *daytime* are divided into syllables between "sun"
    and "light" and "day" and "time" because:
    a. "sun" and "day" are prefixes.
    b. *sunlight* and *daytime* are compound words.
    c. "sun" and "day" are suffixes.
    d. none of the above.

20. The word *return* is divided in the following way:
    a. re/ turn   c. retu / rn
    b. ret / urn   d. none of the above.

Diagnostic Checklist for Word Recognition Skills (Levels 1-4)

Student's Name:

Grade :

Teacher:

	YES	NO	SOMETIMES
1. The student uses:			
a. context clues.			
b. picture clues (graphs, maps, charts).			
2. The student asks someone to state the words.			
3. The student uses the dictionary to try to unlock unknown words.			
4. The student uses phonics analysis by recognizing:			
a. consonants			
(1) single consonants: initial, final			
(2) consonant blends (clusters) (*br, sl, cl, st,* and so on)			
(3) consonant digraphs (*th, sh, ph, ch,* and so on)			
(4) silent consonants (*kn, gn, pn*)			
b. vowels			
(1) short vowels (*cot, can, get,* and so on)			
(2) long vowels (*go, we, no,* and so on)			
(3) final silent *e* (*bake, tale, role*)			
(4) vowel digraphs (*ea, oa, ee, ai,* and so on)			
(5) diphthongs (*oi, oy*)			
c. the effect of *r* on the preceding vowel.			
d. special letters and sounds (*y, c, g, q*).			
e. word families (*an, at, et, un, all, ake, ag, am, ain, ame, ay, en, ick, at, ate, ing, ill, ock, ent, ell, est, in,* and *y*).			
5. The student is able to apply the following syllabication rules to words:			
a. vowel consonant/consonant vowel rule (*vc/cv*) (*but/ter, can/dy*).			
b. vowel/consonant vowel rule (*v/cv*) (*na/tive, ba/by*).			
c. special consonant *le* rule (*vc/cle*) or (*v/cle*) (*ca/ble, can/dle*).			

Answers

Answers to Skill 1 Special Letters and Sounds

Practice 1 (p.38)
Put a line under the following words: dry; why; my; fry; shy; sly; cry.

Practice 2 (p.39)
1. dry; 2. shy; 3. cry; 4. try; 5. Why; 6. fly; 7. My; 8. pry.

Practice 3 (p.40)
Put a line under the following words: pretty; salty; cherry; dirty; muddy; sorry; merry; daddy; berry; bury; penny.

Practice 4 (p.41)
1. berry; 2. bury; 3. happy; 4. fluffy; 5. cherry; 6. party; 7. silly; 8. chilly.

Practice 5 (p.42)
Put a circle around the following words: bunny; fluffy; silly; baby; very; puppy; sunny; dirty; any; penny; baggy; candy; pretty.
Put a line under the following words: why; fly; my; by; fry; sky; cry; pry; shy; try; dry.

Practice 6 (p.43)
Put a circle around the following words: sunny; Mary; merry; sandy; candy; muddy; sleepy; silly; dirty; puppy; bury; sorry; Andy; Molly; pony; bunny.
Put a line under the following words: shy; cry; why; sky; try.
Put an X on the following words: pay; hay; tray; may; pray; play; bray.

Practice 7 (p.44)
1. penny; 2. cherry; 3. fly; 4. bunny; 5. baby; 6. forty; 7. donkey; 8. puppy; 9. thirty; 10. money.

Practice 8 (p.45)
1. sunny; 2. away; 3. shy; 4. easy; 5. cry; 6. baby; 7. why; 8. sorry; 9. very; 10. early; 11. lonely; 12. puppy; 13. Molly; 14. only; 15. silly; 16. happy.

Practice 9 (p.46)
1. silly; 2. bunny; 3. happy; 4. Shy; 5. puppy; 6. sky; 7. sunny; 8. dirty; 9. sixty; 10. jelly.

Practice 10 (p.47)
Put a line under the following words: face; cement; cent; celery.
Put a circle around the following words: cave; carrot; cake; candy; cook; cold.

Practice 11 (p.48)
Put a line under the following words: nice; race; face; place; cement; pencil.

Practice 12 (p.49)
Put a circle around the following pictures: pencil; fence; mice; face; ace.

Practice 13 (p.50)
See children's completed sheets.
1. face; 2. ace; 3. pencil; 4. cake; 5. branch; 6. ice; 7. cat; 8. carrot.

Practice 14 (p.51)
1. carrot; 2. ice; 3. cereal; 4. slice; 5. cake; 6. lace; 7. center; 8. race; 9. place; 10. space.

Practice 15 (p.52)
Put a line under the following words: George; gym; giant; gem.
Put a circle around the following words: gold; golf; get; gone; goat; gown.

Practice 16 (p.53)
Put a line under the following words: gym; giraffe; gem; George; giant; cage; page.

Practice 17 (p.54)
Put a circle around the following pictures: cage; giraffe.
Put a line under the following pictures: goat; gum; eagle; leg; rag; rug.

Practice 18 (p.55)

See children's completed sheets.

1. giraffe; 2. rug; 3. cage; 4. gate;
5. dog; 6. goat; 7. gum; 8. igloo.

Practice 19 (p.56)

1. fog; 2. game; 3. giant;
4. George; 5. dog; 6. get;
7. cage; 8. giraffe; 9. goat;
10. gentle.

Practice 20 (p.57)

1. question mark; 2. zipper;
3. queen; 4. quarter; 5. quilt;
6. giraffe; 7. carrot; 8. goat.

Practice 21 (p.58)

1. carrots; 2. quarters; 3. quart;
4. queen, king or king, queen;
5. Quack; 6. quiet; 7. quilt;
8. question mark; 9. quick

Practice 22 (p.59)

Put a line under the following
words: car; sir; bird; barn; bark;
far; burn; star.

Answers to Skill 2 Syllabication

Practice 1 (p.80)

Put a line under the following:
cra; cot; pen; bal; ban; my;
dol; snow; be; fly.

Practice 2 (p.81)

Write the number 1 for the
following: pick; pill; nut; cut;
dog; dance; drive; call.
Write the number 2 for the
following: peanut; pumpkin;
chestnut; reason; player;
dancing; driver.

Practice 3 (p.82)

Write the number 1 for the
following: dram; foat; broat;
cham; choi; che; dra; drale.
Write the number 2 for the
following: dramete; broato;
cratoi; slery; pignut; broteam;
slickete.

Practice 4 (p.83)

Put one line under the following
words: draw; deck; sign; fly; go;
chase; dress; down; drown.
Put two lines under the following
words: table; tired; parent; carrot;
signal; dreamer.

Practice 5 (p.84)

Put one line under the following:
cro; crad; ded; pli; plem; drime;
blim; kol; quoi; poy.
Put two lines under the following:
crono; dramet; protom; breteme;
pomle.

Practice 6 (p.85)

2. mir / ror; 3. but / ter;
5. win / dow; 6. bar / ber;
8. ten / der; 9. com / ment;

10. can / dy; 12. gar / bage;
13. cor / ner; 14. par / don.

Practice 7 (p.86)

1. rea / son; 2. pi / lot;
6. po / lice; 7. poi / son;
11. la / zy; 12. ba / by;
13. cra / zy; 15. fa / vor.

Practice 8 (p.87)

1.bun / dle; 2. cra / dle;
3. bot / tle; 4. sad / dle;
8. bea / gle; 9. daz / zle;
10. spar / kle; 13. pur / ple;
15. sam / ple.

Practice 9 (p.88)

1. pi / lot; 2. can / dy;
3. brace / let; 4. slip / per;
5. bun / dle; 6. par / don;
7. pil / low; 8. sea / son;
9. muz / zle; 10. pud / dle;
11. mir / ror; 12. dir / ty;
3. o / pen; 14. an / kle;
15. win /ner.

Practice 10 (p.89)

1. gar / bage (1); 2. a / ble (3);
3. pu / pil (2); 4. han / dle (3);
5. mas / ter (1); 6. col / lar (1);
7. pro / nounce (2); 8. nim / ble (3);
9. gig / gle (3); 10. hob / by (1)
11. mir / ror (1); 12. ma / ple (3);
13. bea / con (2); 14. ea / ger (2);
15. pep / per (1).

Practice 11 (p.90)

1. el / bow (1); 2. pi / lot (2);
3. shuf / fle (3); 4. wrin / kle
(3);
5. bu / gle (3); 6. la / zy (2);
7. ti / ger (2); 8. per / son (1);
9. bun / dle (3); 10. ba / by (2);
11. rea / son (2); 12. cor / ner
(1); 13. ta / ble (3); 14. a / corn
(2);
15. af / ter (1).

Practice 12 (p.91)

1. bor / row (1); 2. car / go (1);
3. na / ture (2); 4. tai / lor (2);
5. ri / fle (3); 6. cap / tain (1);
7. pur / pose (1);
8. sim / ple (3);
9. am / ble (3);
10. tan / gle (3);
11. no / tice (2);
12. i / ron; (2);
13. pur / ple (3);
14. par / ty (1);
15. fol / low (1).

Practice 13 (p.92)

1. pro / gram; 2. star / dom;
3. shame / ful; 4. com / bat;
5. rai / sin; 6. la / zy; 7. cor / ner;
8. traf / fic; 9. wrin / kle;
10. gig / gle; 11. af / ter;
12. pep / per; 13. bun / dle;
14. hob / by; 15. shuf / fle.

Practice 14 (p.93)

1. pro / deat; 2. da / ble;
3. sla / peme; 4. bram / mle;
5. shoi / tem; 6. trip / teme;
7. choa / man; 8. fai / mat;
9. cra / mo; 10. tro / tem.

Practice 15 (p.94)

1. den / tist; 2. pro / gram;
3. man / ner; 4. ba / by;
5. re / treat; 6. ta / ble;
7. pa / rade; 8. be / lieve;
9. bun / dle; 10. cra / dle.

Practice 16 (p.95)

1. proi / team; 2. star / pon;
3. sha / mete; 4. slay / mene;
5. dor / let; 6. nai / mem;
7. poi / ler; 8. boi / mer;
9. sla / doil; 10. da / tem.

Practice 17 (p.96)

1. cla / meat´; 2. proi´ / dem;
3. to´ / mar; 4. con / toat´;
5. drom´ / ter; 6. su / reat´;
7. broi´ / man; 8. flag / mene´;
9. mo´ / do; 10. zam / poit´.

Practice 18 (p.97)

1. pro´ / test; 2. la´ / dy;
3. mit´ / tens; 4. can´ / dle;
5. i´ / ron; 6. man´ / ners;
7. re / place´; 8. mon´ / key;
9. can´ / dy; 10. pen´ / ny.

Practice 19 (p.98)

1. cot´ / ton; 2. traf´ / fic;
3. la´ / zy; 4. rum´ / ble;
5. sil´ / ly; 6. sad´ / dle;
7. bot´ / tom; 8. blis´ / ter;
9. mai´ / den; 10. re / peat´.

Answers to Skill 3 Word Families (Phonograms)

Practice 1 (p.113)

1. sap; 2. lap; 3. snap; 4. cap;
5. wrap; 6. slap; 7. nap; 8. chap;
9. trap; 10. clap.

Practice 2 (p.114)

1. map; 2. strap; 3. cap; 4. clap;
5. lap; 6. trap.

Practice 3 (p.115)

1. lap; 2. map; 3. nap; 4. scrap;
5. wrap; 6. snap; 7. clap; 8. cap;
9. strap; 10. trap.

Practice 4 (p.116)

Answers will vary.

Practice 5 (p.117)

1. silly; 2. not silly; 3. not silly;
4. not silly; 5. silly; 6. silly;
7. silly; 8. silly;
9. not silly; 10. not silly.

Practice 6 (p.118)

1. late; 2. Kate; 3. date; 4. gate;
5. hate; 6. plate; 7. skate; 8. state;
9. mate; 10. crate.

Practice 7 (p.119)

1. crate; 2. Kate; 3. gate; 4. plate;
5. skate; 6. date; 7. state.

Practice 8 (p.120)

1. ate; 2. fate; 3. gate; 4. crate;
5. Kate; 6. plate; 7. date; 8.
skate; 9. state; 10. hate.

Practice 9 (p.121)

Answers will vary.

Practice 10 (p.122)

1. silly; 2. not silly; 3. not silly;
4. not silly; 5. not silly; 6. silly;
7. silly; 8. silly; 9. not silly;
10. not silly.

Practice 11 (p.123)

1. wing; 2. ring; 3. king;
4. bring; 5. sling; 6. spring;
7. string; 8. sting; 9. swing;
10. thing.

Practice 12 (p.124)

1. ring; 2. swing; 3. earring;
4. string; 5. wing; 6. king;
7. sling.

Practice 13 (p.125)

1. ring; 2. spring; 3. wring;
4. king; 5. wing; 6. sting;
7. swing; 8. string; 9. sling;
10. fling.

Practice 14 (p.126)

Answers will vary.

Practice 15 (p.127)

1. silly; 2. not silly; 3. not silly;
4. not silly; 5. silly; 6. silly;
7. silly; 8. not silly; 9. silly;
10. not silly.

Practice 16 (p.128)

1. Jill; 2. pill; 3. ill; 4. gill;
5. mill; 6. chill; 7. hill; 8. skill;
9. drill; 10. thrill.

Practice 17 (p.129)

1. silly; 2. silly; 3. silly; 4. silly;
5. silly; 6. not silly; 7. silly;
8. silly; 9. not silly; 10. not silly;
11. silly; 12. not silly.

Practice 18 (p.130)

1. will; 2. thrill; 3. chill; 4. pill;
5. ill; 6. spill; 7. bill; 8. drill;
9. still; 10. hill.

Practice 19 (p.131)

1. lock; 2. sock; 3. clock;
4. knock; 5. dock; 6. flock;
7. frock; 8. stock; 9. rock;
10. smock.

Practice 20 (p.132)

1. silly; 2. silly; 3. not silly;
4. silly; 5. silly; 6. not silly;
7. not silly; 8. not silly; 9. silly;
10. not silly.

Practice 21 (p.133)

1. stock; 2. frock; 3. dock;
4. clock; 5. knock; 6. smock;
7. block; 8. sock; 9. rock;
10. lock.

Practice 22 (p.134)

1. bent; 2. Kent; 3. cent; 4. gent;
5. sent; 6. went; 7. scent;
8. spent; 9. rent; 10. lent.

Practice 23 (p.135)

1. bent; 2. cent; 3. tent; 4. dent;
5. rent; 6. scent; 7. sent; 8. went;
9. lent; 10. spent.

Practice 24 (p.136)

1. well; 2. sell; 3. bell; 4. fell;
5. jell; 6. dwell; 7. swell;
8. spell; 9. smell.

Practice 25 (p.137)

1. yell; 2. shell; 3. jell 4. tell;
5. well; 6. spell; 7. bell; 8. smell;
9. fell; 10. sell.

Practice 26 (p.138)

1. west; 2. guest; 3. best; 4. nest;
5. test; 6. pest; 7. vest; 8. chest.

Practice 27 (p.139)

1. vest; 2. west; 3. best; 4. guest;
5. pest; 6. test; 7. chest; 8. nest;
9. rest.

Practice 28 (p.140)

1. win; 2. thin; 3. kin; 4. fin;
5. tin; 6. twin; 7. chin; 8. skin;
9. grin; 10. shin.

Practice 29 (p.141)

1. spin; 2. shin; 3. twin; 4. thin;
5. in; 6. skin; 7. win; 8. pin;
9. grin; 10. fin.

Practice 30 (p.142)

1. shy; 2. sky; 3. fly; 4, why;
5. try; 6. fry; 7. dry; 8. my;
9. pry; 10. sly.

Practice 31 (p.143)

1. my; 2. sky; 3. cry; 4. fry;
5. fly; 6. dry; 7. sly; 8. shy;
9. pry; 10. spy.

c. oy—it's not a vowel digraph;
you hear both vowels; it's, a
diphthong.
d. shom—you do not hear both
consonants; *sh* is not a blend; it's
a consonant digraph.
e. sar—the vowel is not short; it'
r-controlled.

Part II

1. a; 2. b; 3. a; 4. d; 5. c;
6. a; 7. b; 8. d; 9. b; 10. d;
11. d; 12. b; 13. d; 14. c; 15. a;
16. a; 17. b; 18. a; 19. b;
20. a.

Answers to Special Diagnostic Phonics Assessment

Part I

1. a. drut / ter;   b. ca / dy;
c. thod / man;   d. mad / dle;
e. trot / mer;   f. min / ter.

2. a. fo—it doesn't end in a
consonant; it's an open syllable.
b. le—it doesn't have a consonant
in front of *le* ; it's not a special *le*
syllable.